From the Eye of the Storm

The Experiences of a Child Welfare Worker

Cynthia Crosson-Tower

Harvest Counseling and Consultation

Boston   New York   San Francisco
Mexico City   Montreal   Toronto   London   Madrid   Munich   Paris
Hong Kong   Singapore   Tokyo   Cape Town   Sydney

For James and Muriel, without whose love and support I would not have had the emotional resources to extend a helping hand to others.

Series Editor: *Patricia Quinlin*
Managing Editor: *Karen Hanson*
Editorial Assistant: *Annemarie Kennedy*
Marketing Manager: *Taryn Wahlquist*
Production Administrator: *Marissa Falco*
Electronic Composition: *Publishers' Design and Production Services, Inc.*
Composition and Prepress Buyer: *Linda Cox*
Manufacturing Buyer: *Chris Marson*
Cover Administrator: *Kristina Mose-Libon*

For related titles and support materials, visit our online catalog at www.ablongman.com

Library of Congress Cataloging-in-Publication Data

Tower, Cynthia Crosson.
    From the eye of the storm : the experiences of a child welfare worker / Cynthia Crosson-Tower.—1st ed.
        p.   cm.
    ISBN 0-205-32315-4 (pbk.)
    1. Child welfare.   2. Child welfare workers.   3. Social work with children.
I. Title.
HV713 .T675   2002
362.76′56′092—dc21   2002023220

Printed in the United States of America

 6 7 8 9 10 CRS 07

Contents

Introduction

"But what's it really like, out in the field?" asked Deborah, a student in my fieldwork class that was nearing the end of the semester. " I've taken classes about social work and done my field experience, but what will it be like when I am out there as a social worker working with kids?"

As I considered her question, a flood of memories barraged my mind. What had they been like, those years I spent as a social worker? The success stories and the failures vied for attention as I savored the memories. I hardly realized that Deborah was still speaking. Then, somewhere in the distance, her words filtered through.

"I wish you would write your next book about that. What was it like for you when you started out? What were your cases like? Do you remember any especially? Are there successes?" And so, in a fieldwork seminar that day, this book was born.

At first I contemplated focusing my account on my years as a protective worker, but I soon realized that many of my other experiences made an impact on my protective services experiences. I decided that the students like Deborah would be better served by knowing about other areas of child welfare as well. In addition, everyone's career is unique. The experiences that I had were unique to me as influenced not only by my personality, but also by the point in history, the events of the time, and perhaps just the luck of the draw. While no one's experience will exactly replicate mine, it is helpful to look at a representative career to answer the question of what working in children's services will entail.

The age of the computer, decreased government spending for social services, and a shift in priorities has altered the field of social services, but the needs of people remain similar.

The role of a social worker, especially in children's services, can be filled with excitement, danger, pain, and satisfaction, but rarely ever peace. The turbulence of working with families whose lives are in chaos reminds us how important it is to find peace in our own private spheres. Sometimes it feels like we are in the eye of the storm, the calm part of a whirlwind that gives us a brief moment to breathe before the turmoil begins again. But how vital that eye is for renewal and even survival in this profession!

In writing this account of the experiences of a social worker, I find that time, the great reorganizer, has distorted my memory to some extent. For the most part, I have recounted my reality as I remember it. I have changed the names of most of the people I encountered, both clients and colleagues, out of respect for their privacy. In some instances, I have used composites and altered events slightly, to further protect the privacy of individuals. In addition to recounting how things were, I have tried to point out how the system's policies and procedures may be different today.

By offering this glimpse of my career as a social worker, I extend to Deborah and all of her colleagues who have taught me so much in my twenty-some years of teaching, the gift of sharing that will hopefully answer, to some extent, what it's really like out there.

Acknowledgements

Where does one begin to recognize all those who have shaped a life and career? There are many to whom I owe my understanding of social work, my skills to practice, and my perspective. My appreciation goes especially to Norm LeDoux, Mary McGee, Carel Germaine, Anne Gerstein, Susan McCauley, Joanne Zanotti, Gerry Nugent, Fran McGuinness, and Ted Conna for helping me to develop my skills and understand that people can respond to help if one knows how to reach them. To Lois Buchiane, a more recent mentor and friend who has influenced the writing of this book even though she may not realize it. My thanks once again to Kate Martin, who not only offered me moral support, but took the time to read over the manuscript and make worthwhile suggestions. To all the "Deborahs," my students who, through their questions, reminded me of case after case that had formed me as a social worker. Credit and thanks should also go to Janice Ouellette, my favorite reference librarian, who good-naturedly responds to my crazy requests for information that I needed yesterday. I recognize those clients who, willingly or otherwise, made me a part of their lives. Without them, such a manuscript could never have been written. Although, if I have been successful in disguising their stories to protect their right to confidentiality, they may not recognize themselves.

On a more personal note, my family has been very much a part of this writing by indulging me as I once again sought to meet a deadline. My thanks to Chay, Jamie, Andrew, Nana, and Jim, who put up with a bit less of me while I was busy writing. Finally, I think back with appreciation on all that my father taught me about writing, about people, and about life. I miss him, and believe that he would be proud of my continued efforts as I follow in his footsteps as an author.

1

Where Does it Begin?

How often adults ask little children, "What do you want to be when you grow up?" Has any child ever responded, "a social worker"? I doubt that most children, at least those whose parents or relatives are not in the profession, or whose lives have not been touched by the services of such a professional, would even know what a social worker was. I probably did not. When I was a child in the 1950s, the classic answer for a girl was "a teacher or a nurse." How fortunate we are that those choices, although still laudable, have been joined by many others. I knew that I did not want to be a teacher or a nurse. As a young child I wrote a myriad of stories. It is probably not surprising that this would shape one of my careers. I also watched my minister father and may have had an inkling in that direction, but that was not a profession for women in those days. My parents may have suspected that I would take to the stage, given my ability to "turn on the waterworks" (as my father used to call my tears) or entertain the various adults that peopled my only-child world.

My first attraction to a career came when I took a job as a counselor at a camp for what were then called underprivileged children. Not quite sixteen, I had tired of my summers picking apples or just enjoying myself, and had begged my parents to allow me to take this job. What a culture shock! I remember one little girl, of whom I had become quite fond, giving her address as Canal Street in a nearby city. I knew enough of Canal Street to know that it was lined with abandoned factory buildings and not much else. When I questioned her, I discovered that her itinerant family had squatted in one such building and now considered it to be their own private habitat. Well before the days that homelessness became a public issue, this girl saw nothing wrong with her family's living situation. I also remember tousling the hair of an adorable little boy when he entered camp, only to see him hours later with his head coated with the telltale white powder that was the camp nurse's remedy for lice. My first education in Spanish, knowledge so vital to the field today, came at the hands of several other children who thought it amusing to teach me words that were later to bring a blush to the face of a Spanish-speaking friend. She suggested that I might want to improve my Spanish vocabulary by using textbooks instead of streetwise kids.

My experience that summer opened my eyes to people who had never figured prominently in my sheltered upbringing. Little did I realize that they would play a large role in my later career.

My next summer was spent at a camp for disabled children. It was equally rewarding, and as I watched the often troubled parents of wheelchair dependent children whose lives might soon end, I envisioned myself someday helping these parents cope with their unplanned and often unwanted roles. I had no way of knowing then that I would someday take my place among them as the mother of a disabled child.

After my experiences as a teen, one might expect that I would have realized that I was destined to become a social worker. But the road to social work was, according to my college, through psychology. The fact that my first course in introductory psychology was both boring and devastating to my already shaky grade point average, may have accounted for the fact that I sought out other careers. When I emerged from college with a better grade point average than early courses suggested and my high ideals intact, it was with a dual degree in Religion and Theatre, majors that hardly prepared me for the real world. In retrospect, my majors may have actually served me well. In social work, one needs to be a bit of an actor, and certainly one needs to believe that a higher power will sustain one through the valleys shadowed by hostile, abusive parents and the dangerous streets.

My decision to become a social worker should have been a moment of revelation. In fact, it was a somewhat serendipitous event based on the need for a car. After I graduated and spent a summer as a waitress and a companion to an older woman, I decided that it was time to find a real job. The newspaper and various parental contacts helped me find several positions that I believed that I could fill. I finally narrowed them down to two: a reporter for the local city paper or a social worker for the Department of Public Welfare, Division of Child Guardianship. The reporter's job required that I have a car, a step that finances had not as yet allowed. But the social worker job was in Boston, and I was assured that I could take public transportation. So my career as a social worker was launched on my not having a car. Interestingly enough, it only took several weeks after I began my job to learn that I would be assigned to an office nearer to my parents' home, a rural area, necessitating a car. My only use of public transportation was once a week when I parked my newly acquired car (with Dad's co-signature on the loan, of course) on the outskirts of Boston and rode the MBTA, Boston's subway, to the Central Office for my obligatory supervision and day in Central Office. I never used public transportation to visit clients.

I had started my search for a new job in September. Before the days of the computer and job searches, one was relegated to perusing the paper, writing letters and making phone calls until that coveted first interview became a reality. My final interview opportunity finally came in mid-October, when both the newspaper and the social service agency invited me to meet with a representative. The newspaper was first. Although it seemed like the job might be interesting, I was anxious for my next interview.

The Division of Child Guardianship Area Office was situated in a long block of office buildings in the heart of the city, about an hour from my home. The building was old and a bit dirty, and my ride up in the elevator did not inspire my confidence in the working conditions. When I arrived, the office director was not quite ready, so the receptionist suggested that I go into the workers' room and talk to the social workers.

The workers' room consisted of a very large room populated by desks placed every few feet from one another in three rows. There appeared to be several workers sharing each phone, and some waited impatiently for their colleagues to finish a call. Others sat at desks, busily writing. A few chatted in groups. Everyone seemed in possession of a little black book, which I was to learn was of great importance in the work of the social worker. The small black notebook was used to record information on cases, notes and expense logs. In addition, since most social workers carried them, this career symbol also provided some protection in unsafe neighborhoods. Because these books were carried by both social services and public welfare workers, people in these neighborhoods never knew if the social worker was from public assistance and possibly bringing a check. As a result, there was an unwritten street code that one did not take the chance of biting the hand that fed. Thus, workers learned to carry their books wherever they went. Today, with the advent of the computer and the deterioration of safety, social workers have no such symbol to protect them.

As I stood there surveying my possible future surroundings, one worker approached me.

"Hoping to get a job here?" he said, as if he already knew the answer. "You must be a real masochist!"

I must have looked startled by his evaluation of his job, for he broke into a big reassuring smile and said, "I'm sorry. It's really not that bad!"

His reassuring words were interrupted by another worker, who was peering out a second story window into the old deserted factory building across the street.

"There goes Lolly!" she looked at her watch. "Let's clock it everybody: October sixteenth. Nine months from today, she will be in here to give this one up."

Puzzled, I glanced at my host, who appeared to be somewhat embarrassed.

"You'll have to forgive Beth," he apologized. "We have this client who uses that factory as her personal hotel room for her. . . ." He cleared his throat and glanced at me. It was 1966 and he was unsure of my response to any particularly graphic language. ". . . Amorous activities," he continued carefully. "She invariably becomes pregnant and gives the child up for adoption. She never gets prenatal care and we never know until she delivers. Then she almost drops the baby on our doorstep and we have to place it. Beth has gotten assigned the cases for the last three babies. She's a bit cynical."

"The last three?" I asked. "Can no one work with her?"

He snorted, "Sure, if we could find her! She just disappears." In later years, I was to place one of Lolly's babies and I came to understand why Beth had reacted as she had. At that point, however, I had serious questions about the sensitivity of my potential coworkers. I would soon learn that it is not always easy to understand why people, often hurt by their own dysfunctional childhoods, neglect their children.

The receptionist was at the door announcing that the Director could see me now. Unlike students today, our classes did not prepare us for how an interview would proceed, how to present ourselves, or even how to dress. I was fortunate: my professional parents were well aware of how to impress a potential employer and prepared me for my interview. When I work with fieldwork students today, I help them to anticipate some of the questions they might be asked and how to respond to two-edged questions like "what are your weaknesses?" My teachers did not prepare me in the same manner.

I was lucky in this interview. Reg Forrester, the director of this region, was an affable and well-liked administrator who enjoyed people and was good at his job. Short and balding, with a smile that lit his round face and made his eyes sparkle, Reg was by no means intimidating. He quickly made me forget my questions about the scene I had just witnessed. As he outlined the work I would be doing, he made it sound inviting and enjoyable. He appealed to the idealist that directs each one of us toward the field of social work. I do not remember much about his questions of me. He seemed confident that I would like the job and seemed to think I was a likely candidate. Jubilantly, I left the office, sure that I would be hired.

When the call came the next day that the newspaper wanted me to begin that next Monday, I was almost disappointed. I must have said that I would get back to them, for no sooner had I hung up the phone when Reg Forrester called with the offer of a position as a social worker. I would be starting in mid-November, giving me an additional month to be nervous about how well I could do the job. He also told me that I would not be working in the office near home. Rather, I would be stationed in the Boston office and would cover this area. They had decided to place me in the centralized adoption unit.

For the next month I considered my options. Would I get an apartment in Boston and come out to make my visits in this area? Would I live at home and commute to Boston? No matter how I did it, it became obvious that I would need a car after all. Not too patiently I awaited my first day of work. I still remember it well. On November fourteenth, my Dad took me to the home of another social worker (I had not yet purchased the car, because I needed to establish that I had a paycheck to get a loan) and together we carpooled into Boston. I was nervous and filled with idealism and, I soon discovered, overdressed as I began my career as a social worker in child welfare services. It was to begin thirty-five years to date of satisfying and sometimes frustrating work in the field and teaching in one of the world's most varied and vital professions.

Questions for Thought _____

1. What experiences have you had throughout your life that have suggested that you might enjoy social work?

2. What would you have told the well-meaning adult who asked you what you wanted to be when you grew up? How far have you come from that answer?

3. Looking back over any job you might have had as a child or adolescent, was there anything that suggested that you might go into social work?

4. How did your family feel about social work as a career choice? Did that influence you in any manner?

5. What do you see as the pros and cons of being a social worker?

6. How might you have responded to Beth's comments about Lolly?

7. What types of questions might a potential employer ask? How might you respond?

2

Getting into the Job

I was glad that Dad let me off and bid farewell before Zach, my future coworker, ushered me to his car, a very old gray convertible that was parked on the street near his house. Rust was its predominant body feature, and I secretly wondered if it was held together with masking tape. When the engine finally started with a rheumatic gasp and choke, I had visions of being stranded on the roadside before we ever reached Boston. The one commendation for the old relic was an overactive heater that compensated for the effects of the cold air that flowed freely through the holes in the convertible top. I snuggled down into my coat wondering at the same time if my feet would catch on fire.

"I'm getting a new one, a car," Zach broke into my obviously transparent thoughts. "I've been piecing this old gal together since high school. It used to run pretty well." With a twinkle in his eye, he continued: "I call her the Old Gray Mare".

Suddenly aware of the joke, I laughed. "I know. She's not what she used to be!" The ice had been broken by an arthritic car that groaned as much as her human counterpart might have in a similarly decayed condition, as we turned onto the Massachusetts Turnpike. I began to believe that if Zach was confident that we would make it, I could be too. I sat back and gave in to my excitement and exhilaration about the first day at my new job.

Zach chatted easily, saying first that he had been looking at cars and hoped to get one this week and then talking about the job. I was surprised to learn, as he filled me in on what I could expect, that he had been hired only a month before.

"Adoption is the positive side of this work," he told me, seeming knowledgeable. "You get to be part of the happy ending. It's nice to see kids who might not have had the greatest life end up with folks who may have waited years for children and really want to give them a good home. Don't get me wrong: a lot of the birth parents want the best for their kids too, but they may not be able to keep it together as parents."

I listened, trying to take it all in. I was anxious to begin meeting these people.

"You sound as though you really like this job already. Have you always been interested in social work?"

Zach chuckled and hesitated for a minute.

"Well," he said finally, "I guess I had better let you in on a little secret, since we will be working together. I am actually studying to be a priest. I mean, I was . . . or I am still. I don't know. As the oldest son in a good Catholic family, I've been destined for the priesthood since I was in diapers."

"A priest!"

"Now before you panic and get all weird with me," he began, "let me finish. I am in seminary but it hasn't felt right for a while. Finally, I talked to my advisor and he suggested that I take a year off, get a job, and see how I feel about continuing. I have only been at this job for a month, but it really feels right." He glanced at me tentatively. "Changed your opinion of me?"

Now it was my turn to chuckle.

"I guess I just have to promise not to make any passes at you," I joked. I was soon to learn that Zach was not alone. In fact, my future supervisor would be a former seminarian and during my years in social work, I met several colleagues who were formerly priests or nuns. Perhaps this was to be expected in a predominantly Catholic area, or perhaps social work was a natural profession for someone who wanted to help others but had become disenchanted with the monastic or religious life.

Zach chatted on about himself and the job, and I found myself relaxing. He would later become a good friend who never failed to liven up any gathering with his delightful sense of humor and affable manner. In fact, he did not return to the seminary. At a college reception years later I would meet the woman that he eventually married, not surprisingly another social worker. But I am thankful to Zach for punctuating my first day with his easy talk and big brother manner.

When we finally made it to Boston amidst the morning traffic that I would never grow used to, Zach instructed me where to park and what streets to avoid. I tried to take mental notes, but having lived in a small town since I was in my early teens, it seemed a bit overwhelming.

The Central Office of the Department was located deep in the heart of the "combat zone," an area that was notorious across the state for its pornography stores, x-rated movie houses and people looking for the sexual pleasures provided by the prostitutes who miraculously appeared after dark (One of my faculty colleagues in my current life delights in teasingly announcing to students that I used to work in the "combat zone," and then allowing their imaginations to take over!). Our offices were on the fourth floor of a large archaic building that housed a variety of offices. The Department of Public Welfare occupied the entire floor with the assistance payments section in one wing and the Division of Child Guardianship in the other.

Zach ushered me into our section and once again I was greeted by the rows of desks that characterized the working atmosphere of all the state social service offices. I can never fully understand why it is assumed that the "open concept" is the best working atmosphere for social workers. Granted, it does allow you to keep in close contact with your fellow workers, but the noise level and the distractions are incredible (I will say that I developed an ability to concentrate that has put me in good stead for my writing amidst a variety of distractions.). Apparently, the planners are still convinced about the efficiency of such offices because they still exist. Many are organized into units of bays with five or six desks, but workers still compete for space, and private interviewing rooms are still at a premium.

Along the side walls of our section were a series of offices assigned to the more privileged supervisors. At the far end were the administrative offices where directors could look out on the entire room and assess the industriousness of all who were in the office that day.

Zach enthusiastically introduced me to Herb, his supervisor to whom I had also been assigned.

"He's one of us," Zach winked at me, indicating that I had just met another who had been deterred from a career as a Catholic priest. In fact, Herb had left the priesthood several years before and had subsequently completed a Master's of Social Work program. This explained why all the newest workers were being assigned to him.

Herb was tall, bespectacled, and smiley, and I liked him immediately. It was obvious that he was a bit nervous about his new authority, but dealt with it by acting a bit fatherly. Deirdre, Scott, and Samantha made up the rest of my unit. They were the new kids just like I was. Deirdre was a tall, beautiful young woman, a bit older than the rest of us. Her husband was an executive in the city, and his family had gained prominence and some financial standing. I suspected from her clothes and appearance that Deirdre hardly needed to work, and I suspected that her in-laws may have taken a dim view of the profession she had chosen. Deirdre was quite down-to-earth and almost embarrassed by her wealth. As she continued to shop at discount clothes stores, she admitted to more humble roots and complained that she could not get used to not watching out for a bargain.

Scott was someone I would never know well. He was serious and retiring, and left for the business world less than a year after we began working together. He was to cover the geographic area slightly west of mine and I would have liked to get to know him better. He was very involved with his wife and new baby, and had no time for socializing. Samantha, or Sammi as she liked to be called, was a free spirit. She always provided a new surprise in what she did or how she viewed situations. We were to have some fun times together, visiting her home in Maine and enjoying the ocean. She too left after a year. I suspect that of those who met together that day, it was only Zach and I who continued in the field of social services for an entire career.

Burnout is not uncommon in the field. One statistic says that most social workers are at their jobs for an average of two years. Many leave, lured by more attractive salaries and discouraged by the working conditions and often uncooperative clients. I have found that the highs can be monumental and they compensate to some degree for the myriad of lows. I have never regretted my choice of profession, and many who have remained in the field would agree. There is something about knowing that you have touched someone's life in a positive way that makes it all worthwhile.

In those days, training was literally on-the-job. Today, mercifully, most states give their social workers training that may last from a week to several weeks. But at that time, our first supervisory meeting involved being assigned our first cases that we were expected to begin seeing that same week. Our training consisted of shadowing another worker to see how things were done. I was overjoyed when Herb suggested that I might accompany Zach, who had several visits that week. It never occurred to me that Zach had only been on the job a month himself. I just assumed that somehow, he had the whole routine down and was a good model. Later in the week, I was to be invited to go out with several other workers and I would discover that Zach had indeed taken to his new role quickly and effortlessly.

Having assigned me several cases and arranging for us to be shown the ropes by Zach and several other coworkers, my supervisor oriented his new recruits to the office and various other staff members. Many of the workers were out in the field, but all of the supervisors and administrators greeted and welcomed us. It was a warm atmosphere despite the stories of some difficult personalities that I was to hear later. The few workers that were in were engaged in phone conversations, reading records, or talking into a Dictaphone.

For children of the computer age, a Dictaphone is tantamount to a dinosaur. One dictated into a mouthpiece and later a secretary would play back your words via headphones and type the entry into a record. Now, all dictation is done on computers, with programs created especially for such dictation and form completion. Not only is it easier for all concerned, but computers allow the offices to communicate statewide for better tracking and client service.

I was to learn the importance of up-to-date dictation, a task that I learned to dislike and avoid. In all my years as a social worker, I was never called to task about anything except procrastination in dictating. I suspect that computer recording has also eliminated some degree of the reluctance that social workers once had to accomplishing this weighty task.

With my head full of names that I was sure that I could never remember tomorrow, I wondered what was next.

"Let's go," said Herb as he herded the four new workers into the elevator. "It's coffee break time."

Not a coffee drinker myself and eager to learn more about the job, I was in no way interested in taking a coffee break, but I followed along as instructed. Today, workers who need some morning sustenance are more likely to be seen at their desks with a take-out cup and perhaps a bag containing some form of morning snack. But at that office, at that time, coffee break was a ritual that everyone observed religiously. I am a chronic workaholic, but when I would later attempt to forgo this morning ritual, my coworkers chastised me for "making the rest of us look bad." In time, I would accept the ritual of coffee break as an inevitable part of being in the office, and a time to take a breath in an otherwise relentless and overwhelming schedule. In later years, I was also to discover that most food was eaten on the run between clients. I learned that I should have been more appreciative of this mid-morning break.

This first coffee break found the five of us crowded around a table for three in a tiny hole-in-the-wall coffee shop tucked in the bowels of the office building. How so many people from various offices all managed to get coffee and return to work before afternoon is a fact that still astounds me, but in no time we had finished our coffee and were ready for more of our first day.

For the remainder of the morning we were instructed to become familiar with a very dull policy manual that told us what we could and couldn't do. Lunch followed, another social affair that, at least for today, included Herb's entire unit, consisting of the four new recruits and Zach. As a group, we traipsed down the street to one of the less greasy looking restaurants that advertised a quick, working man's lunch. As we ate, the repartee between Herb and Zach, who shared similar backgrounds, life experiences, and now a month's worth of working together, kept us all amused. Deirdre, the most outgoing of the new group, joined in with stories about the idiosyncrasies of her somewhat snobbish new in-laws, and we all began to relax in the camaraderie of the group. So engrossed were we in the company that Zach's finding a fly in his entree was more fodder for increased laughter than it was a catastrophic event.

Despite the enjoyable lunch, I looked forward to returning to the office, knowing that the afternoon would be dedicated to reading and discussing my new cases.

Questions for Thought

1. What are the similarities—besides the obvious one of working with people—between professions like the priesthood and social work?

2. How do you approach new work situations? What do you need to feel comfortable?

3. What type of working conditions do you need? Would the working conditions of a large room with various people doing different tasks be difficult for you?

4. Why might people leave social work after only a short period of time?

5. What kind of training do you expect from a job? How would you feel about the "jump-in-and-swim" approach?

6. How are you about documentation? Will keeping regular records come easily for you?

3

A Dose of Reality and Culture Shock

Growing up, I remember a house down the block that had an abundance of children. They always appeared to be extremely dirty, ragged, and very noisy as they scampered about the yard and roamed the neighborhood. They were the kids that neighbors watched, clicking their tongues and shaking their heads. It was rumored that the mother drank and had a child every year, often by different men. I was never sure what the issue was, but I was sure from the whispered comments of the adults in my neighborhood that these were children to be avoided. In my years of working with troubled families, I have learned how many are isolated from their neighbors by the very issues that should be met with compassion and help. Instead, such families remain on the fringes of society, seen daily by social workers that list them among the many on their caseloads. I remembered that such a family had seemed so far out of my own frame of reference. As I read over the cases I had been given, I thought of the neglectful, troubled family I had seen as a child and wondered what had become of them.

When I work with students now, we discuss what is often called culture shock: that initial combination of incredulousness and depression that one feels when coming into contact with families who do not conform to what one believes a family should be. How could someone try to starve their own child, or drink to the exclusion of meeting the child's needs? Why would a mom choose an abusive boyfriend over her own child? How could a father allow his wife to die of a painful disease under the eyes of their children in a remote shack with no water or heat while he left everyday to go to his upscale job in his newly purchased Jaguar? As a social worker, the first time you see how people live and mistreat children, it is indeed a culture shock. As I read over and discussed the first of my cases with my supervisor, I was to experience the culture shock common to new workers. In years to follow, when I had seen all these cases and worse, the children would still tug at my heartstrings. And although it might seem easy to blame the parents, they, although responsible for their children's pain, were often victims of their own private hell. In addition, many had never had the opportunity in

10

their own lives for the love, guidance, and parenting that would prepare them to parent their own children. Not an excuse, just reality.

It was my role as an adoption worker to become familiar with the backgrounds of the children I would be placing for adoption. Many of their files were voluminous. Many had experienced more pain and trauma in their young lives than one could possibly imagine. Gabby was three months old when she had been removed from her birth family. During her first three months, she had been consistently beaten, thrown across the room by Mom's drunken boyfriend, and burned with cigarettes by a mother who could not stand her crying. Now Gabby was three years old. She had been in the same foster home since her separation from her parents, mainly because a judge had felt that they could be rehabilitated. However, despite his faith in them, they had disappeared over a year before.

When parents cannot be found, the Department is forced to file a petition asking that parental rights be terminated so that the child can be placed for adoption. It is a tedious and lengthy process designed to protect the rights of the parents but with the result that a child may remain in limbo long after they should have been placed with a loving adoptive family. Gabby had been caught up in such a situation. Admittedly, she had flourished with an older couple for whom she was the only foster child. Her only residual effect from her horrendous abuse was that if one raised an arm or hand, even in an innocent gesture, Gabby would cringe, afraid that she was about to be hit. This amazed me, as it was clear that the foster parents would never have struck this child, to whom they were so devoted. The plan, my supervisor told me, was to finally place Gabby for adoption now that the court had finally terminated her parents' rights.

"Won't these foster parents be devastated?" I asked.

"I am sure they will," he told me with compassion. "But their health is not the best and they are really in no position to adopt."

I would also learn that, at that time, foster parents were not encouraged to adopt. As one worker put it, "Foster parents expecting to adopt is like going through the back door to adoption. We encourage them to love the kids and let them go."

Although today social workers hope that there will still be folks able to love and nurture children and then let them go, new research into the effects of separation has educated us to the fact that there are times when the stability of being adopted by a foster parent is preferable to another separation. I soon realized that no matter what policy said, Gabby's situation would not be as easy as we anticipated.

"And that brings us to Skipper and ugly Franny," Herb told me as we reviewed my new cases.

" 'Ugly' Franny! That's terrible!" I interjected.

He chuckled. "I'm sorry, but this has got to be the homeliest child I have ever seen. On the other hand, her brother, Skipper, is adorable."

The two children were born of different fathers and an Anglo mother. Skipper's father was Puerto Rican and Franny's father was African American. Mentally ill and itinerant most of her life, their mother had tried to parent them, but her appetite for various men and for heroin meant that they were frequently abandoned or neglected. Skipper had been found at two years, when he had been left behind in a flophouse where drug addicts crashed for a night or two. Franny remained with her mother until she was five and had become a behavior problem. When I met her, I realized why Herb had given her, in the confines of the office, the most uncomplimentary name. Her completion did credit to neither of her racial ancestries but was rather a sallow, yellowish brown. Her hair was an unbecoming natural orange, and her features did nothing to improve her appearance. I often wondered why nature had been so cruel to this young girl who already had so many strikes against her. To her further detriment, Franny's chaotic beginnings had left her sullen, belligerent and temperamental, a combination that did not give her many chances to be placed in an adoptive home. She was seven when I met her, but we never could find an adoptive home to give her the love and stability that she so badly needed. Instead, Franny would bounce from foster home to foster home until she finally aged out of the foster care system.

Skipper was as different from his sister as a child could be. He was handsome in a way that invited him to be used as a poster child. His large dark eyes sparkled with mischief, and his curly dark hair and light bronze complexion made one wonder if he would grow into a popular film star. But it was Skipper's personality that won my heart. At five, he was always ready with a cute comment or a searching question. He was as affectionate as his sister was disagreeable, and was loved by all.

Because the children had been removed from their mother at different times, they were placed in separate foster homes. Although they saw each other, Franny rejected her charming sibling and they never really got to know each other. Thus, the plan was to place them in separate homes.

I also remember Jeremy, a child who had been given up for adoption at birth. At two months old he had suffered from a high fever, which had precipitated a seizure, the only one he would ever have. Because of that seizure, it was felt that he should remain under observation to determine if he should be placed as a child with special needs. Ironically, he had been placed in an overcrowded foster home with a foster mother who had long passed her nurturing prime. At a year old, when I got his case, Jeremy was a withdrawn, uninteresting child who was suspected to be developmentally delayed. Thus, he would be placed as a special needs child.

The last of my initial cases was a healthy five-month-old boy, Billy, who had been released for adoption two weeks earlier by an unwed mother who was finally able to give him up for adoption. He had been placed in a foster home, but the plan was to find an adoptive home for him as soon as possible. Herb assured me that this would be an easy, straightforward case that would give me a feeling of success. The older children and the special needs child might provide more of a challenge in finding a home and in placing them. Little did he know how wrong he would be.

I found that I was emotionally exhausted when Herb and I finished discussing my new cases. As I was feeling somewhat overwhelmed, he explained that I could start on these now, and by the end of next week, he would give me several more. Glancing at my less than confident face, Herb smiled warmly.

"I know," he reassured, "we really throw you into it. I will have Zach and a couple of other workers take you out with them for a few days until you get your feet wet. In the meantime, let's outline exactly what should be done in each of these cases." He pushed a pad and paper toward me and urged me to make a list. I wrote as he spoke.

Gabby

1) Make a visit or several visits to the foster home to assess child's readiness for adoption and her understanding of the fact that an adoptive home is being sought for her. Also, talk with the foster mother about the plan.
2) Check the card-sort to find a suitable adoptive couple interested in a three-year-old girl.
3) Call the couple and present a verbal picture of Gabby to them. If you can get pictures from the foster parents or take one at the visit, bring those.
4) If the couple wants to go forward, arrange for them to meet with Gabby in a neutral setting like a park or restaurant. They should be allowed to observe the child and then be introduced as friends of yours. Then they should be allowed to interact with child.
5) Once the couple decides that Gabby is the child for them, visit the foster home. Assess Gabby's impression of the adoptive couple. Assuming that it is positive, explain to Gabby that she will be visiting her new mommy and daddy.
6) Set up several day visits and then an overnight to culminate in the placement of the child.
7) On the day of the final placement, talk with Gabby and the foster parents about separation.
8) Call the day after the placement to determine how things are going.
9) Complete paperwork transferring the child to the adoptive couple and ending the foster parent's room and board payments for Gabby.
10) Visit at regular intervals (once a week, then every few months) to support the adoptive couple and see how everyone is adjusting.
11) At the end of year, prepare everyone to go to court so that the adoption can be finalized. Complete necessary paperwork.

As we finished this first case, I had developed a hundred questions and was feeling even more overwhelmed. What is a card-sort? Herb explained that it was a system that he had developed to match available children with adoptive parents. A series of cards were punched according to the preferences of the parents. By using the characteristics of the child and a needle-like device, a worker could bring out only the cards of families interested in just this type of child. We thought that it was a wonderful invention, but when I look what the computer has done to simplify the process, I realize what a dinosaur our system was.

I had other concerns, like what if either the parents or the child did not like the match? Herb assured me that this was an unusual occurrence and, in fact, I discovered only one instance in my numerous years as an adoption worker. Chemistry is not always right and when either part of the adoption connection feels uncomfortable, that should be respected.

I had other logistical questions about forms and policies, but Herb assured me that those would be answered when I got to the point of needing them.

Although the adoption process may have changed to some extent and is certainly enhanced logistically by the computer, the initial meeting and connecting is still much the same.

The lists for the other children were much the same. Herb urged me to check with Jeremy's pediatrician to make sure that there were no other medical issues. In addition, he wondered about Franny's attractiveness to an adoptive couple, both because of her appearance but also because of her behavior, or her readiness to be adopted. He would prove to be correct on both counts, and Franny would remain in foster care. Today, Franny might have had a better chance, as couples are a bit more realistic about the ravages of abuse on children, and help for troubled children is more available, though by no means plentiful.

As we were finishing up, a secretary dropped a file carefully on Herb's desk, obviously unmindful of either the closed door or the fact that we were in conference.

"Thank you, Gertie," he intoned with obvious annoyance. She hardly looked at him, but exited muttering to herself. Herb shook his head in resignation.

"If you give a secretary a file to type, you might want to avoid giving it to Gertie, especially if it is a case involving sexual abuse," he warned.

"But why?" I asked.

"You'll see soon enough," he finished dismissively. "Not that we have a choice, though. With the new system, you just put your dictation in the typing box and the next secretary available gets it. Well, maybe you'll be lucky," he said, obviously concluding the interview. "Come on. Let's see if we can arrange for some workers to let you shadow them for a few days."

Questions for Thought _____

1. Do you remember your first culture shock? What was it? How did it affect you?

2. What was your reaction when you read about the cases confronting this new social worker? How would you have felt?

3. How might you have kept the facts of all the cases separate? Would a list, such as the one this worker made, help you?

4. Do you feel comfortable asking questions in new situations? What if your supervisor does not seem receptive to your questions?

5. If you had been this worker, what would you have asked about the cases and the policies of the agency?

4

"The Shadow Knows"

Zach seemed to have no problem agreeing to continue showing me the ropes and we arranged to meet the two mornings later when he would make his first visit of the day. In the meantime, Herb suggested I spend the next several days in the office reading policies and talking to other workers. Although I enjoyed meeting people on Tuesday and Wednesday, I was anxious to get out with Zach and discover what visits were all about.

I asked my family to again drop me off at Zach's, assuring them that I would pick up my new car as soon as I had time to go to the bank with my Dad and sign the loan. It had been inconvenient for my father, who had driven me to Boston for the last two days, but he would never complain. I was sure that he, as much as I, was anxious for me to get my new car.

Zach greeted me with his usual good humor.

"Got a surprise for you!" he laughed, as he led me to a brand new sky blue Mustang parked outside his house.

"Yours?" I asked in obvious envy. I still couldn't imagine being a car owner myself.

He cooed and preened over it in obvious delight.

"I spent a bit more than I had hoped," he confessed. "But it was all worth it. I just got it last night."

As I slid into the luxurious new seat with cloth upholstery, I understood his pride. I imagined that my purchase would by necessity be a lot less costly.

Zach spent the next few minutes fishing around the dashboard and admitted sheepishly, "I still don't know how half the stuff works. Watch me put on the air conditioning instead of the heat!"

We talked easily about the upcoming visit.

"You'll love this foster mom," he assured me with confidence. "She's the greatest." He chuckled at some private joke and then seemed to think he could share it.

"If you promise not to tell at the office, I'll tell you what happened my first day in the field." He continued, "I was scheduled to see this foster mom. I was really nervous, especially about being able to connect with the kids. I have little cousins, but no one has ever just handed me a kid and said, "Here, take him." We have to win them over a bit so that we can take them out and get to know them. That way, when it comes time to take them out to see their new parents, getting them to go with you is a piece of cake."

I imagined that Zach's easy manner and big smile would make him a natural with kids, but continued to listen to his tale.

"Anyway, this foster mom, Mrs. Riley, was the first one I had ever visited. She has a couple of foster kids, but my case is a little girl, Julie, who is almost a year old at that time. When I got there, Julie was napping and Mrs. R. and I talked for a while. Julie got up and Mrs. R. changed her and asked if I'd like to hold her. Panic! But bravely, I took her. She didn't fuss or anything and I was feeling kind of good about that."

Zach fiddled on the dash again until he had the windshield wipers and I realized that a cold mist had started to punctuate the November morning. I hoped that it was too early to freeze and cause problems driving. I would later learn that social workers, like postal workers, are often required to go out regardless of the weather.

"Mrs. R. and I were having a great talk and I relaxed with little Julie. She gurgled and cooed and I thought, 'Boy this is a cinch!' Mrs. R. started looking at me funny, like she wanted to interrupt, but I was talking away. Finally, feeling very competent, I admitted to her that it was my first day and I had been really worried about relating to little kids. She started laughing and couldn't stop and then she managed, 'It looks like you've won Julie over, but what a price!'" Zach started laughing too, and his laughter was infectious.

"What's so funny?" I asked, caught up in his merriment but not knowing the reason.

Zach spoke with difficulty through his laughter.

"When I looked at Julie, feeling so proud of my rapport with her, and that she was so quiet, I understood why Mrs. R. was having a hard time containing herself. There was Julie, bouncing on my knee, with my entire tie stuffed in her mouth!"

The image of baby Julie devouring her novice social worker was all I needed. Our laughter lasted us the better part of our drive to the foster home. As we turned down Mrs. Riley's street, Zach finished his story.

"So you can see how this foster mom and I have a great relationship now. I've had to visit Julie often and I love seeing them both. You are in for a treat." I silently thanked both Herb and Zach for arranging for me to visit this particular home for my first visit. I too was to grow especially fond of Mrs. Riley, who was ready for any mishap and handled them all with humor and warmth.

Zach parked his prized new car on the steep grade right in front of the large picture window of the low, sand-colored modern home. The yard was fenced and well kept with a myriad of child-sized toys dotting the lawn. Mrs. Riley, a large, motherly woman, greeted us enthusiastically at the door. It was obvious that she enjoyed Zach's visits.

"Come on in," she insisted. "I just put some coffee on. Sit yourself down." With that she disappeared into the kitchen. Several children played on the living room floor. A dark-eyed, dark-skinned boy of about five or so eyed me suspiciously from behind a chair. Zach was obviously a regular visitor, but I was someone new and apparently suspect from the child's point of view. A beautiful blonde baby girl, ostensibly the infamous tie-eater, played on the floor. When she saw Zach, she smiled broadly and getting unsteadily to her feet, toddled over to him.

"I assume this is Julie, and I guess you have won her over," I remarked.

"No, she just likes the taste of his ties!" bombed a laughing voice, as Mrs. Riley emerged from the kitchen with a tray filled with a plate of cookies and three cups.

"Oops!" she said, looking not the slightest bit sorry for her comment.

"It's okay," admitted Zach. "I had to tell her about the famous tie-muncher!" He tickled Julie, who giggled with obvious enjoyment. Zach flipped his tie over his shoulder as he suspected that Julie might live up to her reputation. I was later to recognize that women were no less at risk at the hands of strange children. I learned to wear small, simple earrings in my pierced ears after more than one baby had grabbed my large hoops with a painful result.

Zach asked Mrs. Riley how Julie had been while she welcomingly poured coffee and offered cookies. Manuel, the other child, slowly ventured out and began to play with Julie's forgotten blocks, at which point the little girl screeched and struggled out of Zach's lap.

"Now Julie, we must share," soothed Mrs. Riley as she picked up the baby and offered her a cookie. Julie, forgetting her need to reclaim her blocks, mouthed the cookie contentedly with the help of four small teeth.

"We think that we have found an adoptive couple for Julie," Zach began, carefully mindful of the foster mother's obvious attachment to the child. There was a moment when Mrs. Riley's face revealed her underlying feelings of sadness, but then she smiled.

"It's about time you guys got off your duffs and found this cutie a home! Who would want to miss a minute of those smiles?" She hugged Julie playfully, eliciting the smiles in question from the happy child.

"Mrs. Riley has done wonders for Julie," explained Zach. "They say that when she was brought here, she wasn't in great shape."

"That's for sure," added the foster mother in her characteristic manner of always having the last word. "She was two weeks old and I have never seen such a bad diaper rash. I guess the police found her in a drug bust. Everyone was so strung out that no one knew who she belonged to. They finally got one of the girls to admit that she was hers. The mom's been in detox so many times that there is no way that she can take care of this beautiful baby." She rubbed Julie's curly locks fondly.

"She finally signed an adoption surrender two weeks ago," finished Zach. "And it certainly wasn't difficult to find a couple who would like—" Suddenly Zach's face contorted in horror. He leapt from his chair, and with an exclamation bounded out the front door. Mrs. Riley and I exchanged incredulous glances. In the next moment I happened to see, out of the corner of my eye, a streak of blue that I recognized as Zach's precious new car rolling past the end of the window. We dashed outside, to watch

Zach, in hot pursuit, attempt to open the door and jump in. He finally managed this acrobatic feat inches before the car crashed into the stone wall at the far end of Mrs. Riley's sloping, winding street.

The foster mother hoisted Julie on her hip, and grabbing Manuel's hand, ran with me to Zach's side. He was slumped in the driver's seat, one foot still on the brake. His face was white and perspiration dotted his brow.

"Is it all right?" I gasped almost at the same moment as Mrs. Riley said, "Are you okay?"

Zach finally smiled sheepishly. "I guess I should have made sure the emergency brake was on." We all laughed in relief and allowed him to take us back to the front door.

The remainder of the visit was far less exciting. Zach arranged to pick up Julie the next Monday, once he had had a chance to introduce her on paper to the adoptive couple. If they liked what they heard, they would meet her. If the adoption appeared to be a go, Zach suggested that Mrs. Riley talk to Julie about having a Mommy and Daddy for always. We knew how difficult it would be for the aging foster mother, but she gave every indication of wanting what was best for Julie.

Still slightly shaken by his experience, Zach seemed anxious to take his car out on the road to assure himself that it was indeed all right. I felt badly for him. I was sure that he parked the car on the street (as opposed to Mrs. Riley's seemingly safe drive-way) because he wanted to show off his new prize to her. I was glad that the mishap had ended favorably for the new car owner.

Zach announced that we had an hour drive ahead of us, but that we would get some lunch before our next visit. As we drove, Zach seemed pensive.

"Do you think I should get seat covers?" he said suddenly. "I didn't really expect to get cloth upholstery, but the car dealer had this one on the lot and I couldn't resist."

I rubbed the smooth seat beside me in appreciation. It was a lovely fabric.

"I mean, it almost seems like an insult," Zach continued. "I pick up some Mom and her kid to take them to the doctor or something, and here are these vinyl seat covers. It almost seems like I am telling them that I expect them to get my car dirty."

I wasn't sure how to respond. My family's car had usually had factory made vinyl seats, and the idea of whether or not to buy seat covers had not been a part of my decision-making.

"I guess a lot of people with little kids must have seat covers," I offered. "Maybe the clients won't notice one way or the other."

Zach grew pensive again.

"Guess I will just have to think about it," he finished.

We chatted easily for the remainder of the hour until Zach announced that we were nearing the foster home.

"Hamburger okay with you?" he asked, turning into a small restaurant parking lot. Although I suspect that Zach usually found a takeout restaurant and ate on the run, I guessed that he trusted neither of us with his new upholstery, so we ate in the small, crowded restaurant while Zach filled me in on the next case.

"This foster mom just discovered that she has cancer and cannot keep the child she has. This is a three-year-old boy, Jason, and he is really attached to her. It will be tough. We are taking him to another home while the foster mom gets chemotherapy."

"I hope she'll be okay," I said.

"Me too," he agreed.

The mood at the next foster home was understandably solemn. The foster mother was as thin as Mrs. Riley had been robust, and this woman's drawn face and dark rimmed eyes attested to the fact that she was going through a tough time. Jason was ready for our scheduled arrival. He was dressed in overalls and his box of belongings awaited his departure. He glanced at us with disinterest. Perhaps he felt that failing to acknowledge us would deter us from our task of removing him from a home he had grown to love.

"He doesn't feel great today," Mrs. Felice explained to us. "At some level, he knows what's happening." Jason clung to her as she spoke, and there was no doubt that he knew that he was being taken from her. Zach had shared that Jason's birth mother had died of an overdose and Jason's biological father, unable to care for him, had asked the Department to take Jason until he got on his feet. Everyone wondered when that would be, especially since he had ceased his infrequent visits. It was suspected by those familiar with the case that Dad might just disappear in time. In the meantime, a social worker was working with him, but had referred Jason to the adoption unit for an evaluation for future adoption. I thought of the losses that this child had already suffered, and suddenly felt moved with compassion for this small child whose life had already been punctuated by pain.

Zach talked with Mrs. Felice while I tried to engage Jason. He wanted no part of me and turned his head when I spoke to him. Finally, it was time for our departure. Mrs. Felice picked Jason up with an effort that was evidence of her weakened body, kissed him, and handed him to Zach. The little boy took the transfer complacently but huge tears began to run down his small face as Zach took him out to the car and strapped him into a car seat situated in the back seat of his car for this purpose. Jason watched out the window as we drove off, still passive, but weeping silently.

"Situations like this are killer," murmured Zach, so that Jason could not hear. "These kids go through so much that you hate to be the one who adds to the hurt."

I listened but was at a loss for words. How many times in the future would I be forced to take children from the adults they loved?

We drove in silence for a time. Zach kept looking back into the rearview mirror to observe Jason despite the fact that I was also keeping an eye on him. Presently he fell into a deep and blessed sleep, snoring gently as we drove through the countryside.

"I wish I could take him right to a potential adoptive home," Zach said, still in a lowered tone. "But things are too up in the air with Dad. He's not about to sign an adoption surrender when he still thinks he'll be able to take him sometime. Even if we wanted to petition the court to have Dad's rights terminated, his recent interest would get the petition thrown out. And even if that were not the case, the courts are so backed up that it would take almost a year before the petition could be heard and possibly allowed. So, unless Dad decides to sign a surrender very soon, this little guy is looking at a prolonged stay in foster care."

Today, life might be a bit different for a child like Jason. Recognizing a child's need for stability, the Department is now able to place children in what are referred to as at-risk adoptive homes. These are adoptive parents who have agreed to accept a child who may be in some legal risk, understanding that if the parent does not sign a surrender or the court petition is not allowed, they will not be able to adopt. Usually such placements, only made when the social worker is fairly confident that the child will indeed become available for adoption, usually have a positive outcome for the adoptive family. At the same time, they offer the child a few months more of the love and stability that they so desperately need. Occasionally they do not work out, causing pain to all involved, but the availability of such a plan is a benefit in most situations.

Zach tried to take both of our minds off the inequity of Jason's plight by telling me about the forms that would be necessary for him to complete when he returned to the office. Forms are the nightmare of every social worker, although they are somewhat simplified now by being on the computer. Still, no matter how much one enjoys working with people, there are still the inevitable moments when one must complete a myriad of forms so that there is record of a child's whereabouts and the various people who need to be paid are paid. Every such removal or placement would require close to an hour of form completing or, in the eyes of the bureaucracy, it had never happened.

We were nearing the city. Jason was being taken from his rural foster home to one in a residential section of the city. This day, the traffic was heavy and sirens were coming from all directions. An ambulance sped by, hardly giving us time to pull over to allow it to pass. Several police cars came from different directions, the flash of their red and blue lights heralding their urgency.

"There must be an accident," suggested Zach, trying to see ahead of the seemingly endless line of cars.

Suddenly there was a cry from the back seat. The air was pierced with another shriek of urgency as Jason, awakened by the noise and lights and probably disoriented, began to scream and writhe. We tried to comfort him, but he thrashed and screamed louder. Surrounded by the turbulent effects of whatever was before us on the road and unsure of what driving hazard might await us, I hesitated to take the child from his seat. But his thrashing concerned me and I turned to unstrap him and pick him up. As I did, I saw that he had stopped thrashing but was horrified to realize that from the frightened child's mouth spewed vomit that was now slowly cascading onto the seat of Zach's new car. I grabbed the only thing in sight, a half empty Kleenex box, to contain the remainder of the vomit, but had the foresight to grab a handful of the Kleenex for the aftermath. There was no hope of pulling over, due to the traffic. Zach watched in the rear view mirror, hopeless as his new seats became christened by his little passenger.

Jason, drained both physically and emotionally, soon quieted and resumed his complacency with heavy eyes threatening to be overcome once again by sleep. I attempted to mop up what I could. We passed the accident that had slowed our progress and turned up another city street. I looked at the mess of the back seat and my heart went out to little Jason. How he must be hurting, and with no way, other than what had happened involuntarily, for him to cry out for help. As I thought about this, I wondered what his future would hold. Knowing that I could do little more for him at present until we were able to stop and clean him up, I turned to face our continued drive. Then remembering Zach and the impact on his new and beloved car, I glanced furtively at him. His face was as passive as Jason's now was.

"Oh Zach," I said helplessly, "I'm so sorry."

He breathed a sigh of resignation.

"I think I'll get seat covers," he said, as he turned into the driveway of Jason's new foster home.

Questions for Thought

1. Have you had much experience with children? What is, or would be, the biggest challenge about working with children?

2. How good are you at laughing at yourself? What might you have done in Zach's shoes when Julie ate his tie?

3. Zach was in real conflict about the seat covers. How do you know when to protect yourself or your property and when your need to protect is insulting or detrimental to clients?

4. How would you have handled the situation with Mrs. Felice? What might you have said to her?

5. How would you have felt having to move Jason? What might you have done to make the transition easier for him?

5

On My Own

Now that I had shadowed Zach, Millie, and several other workers for several days, I was anxious to get out on my own. I had watched Zach present Julie verbally to the Morrises, who were enthusiastic and anxious to meet her. I had also gone with Millie to court for an adoption finalization. Millie had visited the adoptive couple and the child in the home since the placement, and was confident that all was going well. The petition for the couple to adopt had been brought to probate court and allowed by the judge. Next, the child's name would be changed to that of the adoptive couple, and the original birth certificate would be amended. This was the culmination of a great deal of work on everyone's part, and the moment for which both the adoptive couple and the worker had hoped. It became almost anti-climactic in its simplicity, but most couples followed the brief court visit with some type of celebration to which social workers were often invited. I had been invited to join the family for a picnic, albeit indoor, with cake amidst joyful faces. There were two children involved in the adoption, a two-year-old boy and a four-year-old girl, and I hoped that the residual effects of the background that I had read about in their record would not mar their future. For now, it was a happy scene.

I was so anxious to begin my own cases that I almost resented the Thanksgiving holiday that broke into my work schedule. As we gathered for a big dinner, I realized how thankful I was to be doing a job that would be so rewarding. I thought of the families who might hold me and my agency in their prayers next Thanksgiving as they cared for their new adopted son or daughter.

Returning to the office the next Monday, I assured Herb that I was ready to start on my own. Since my supervisor felt that five-month-old Billy might be the easiest case, I began by making an appointment to see him at his foster home. I then scheduled visits with the foster mothers of Jeremy (1 year old), Skipper (5 years old) and Gabby (3 years old). Herb suggested that I see these children before getting to know Franny, as her foster home was quite far away and her adoption prospects less likely.

I had been on the job for over a week now, and had picked up my new car, a bright red Volkswagen Bug, the day before. I vowed that I would put the emergency brake on when I parked on a hill, and prayed that my experiences with a new car would not mirror Zach's. I also congratulated myself on my choice of vinyl seat covers.

I had ambitiously scheduled a full day of visits. Billy's foster mother greeted me, matter-of-factly stating the number of workers she had had over the years and her acceptance that Billy was one more child who would soon leave. For all I knew about babies, Billy appeared to be a normal 3-month-old. He jabbered appropriately, held my finger, and smiled on cue. His foster mother assured me that he was an average baby who did all the proper things at the proper times. I learned my first lesson about male babies when she asked if I would change him while she tended to a spat between two toddlers who were also in her care. I had had little experience with babies, but had babysat for a neighbor's daughter a few times in my teens. I knew about holding a young baby's head and ensuring that they did not roll off the changing table while I reached for a diaper. What I had not experienced was the propensity of baby boys to perform when the diaper was removed. Thus, Billy introduced himself to me by projecting a stream of urine on my cheek while I reached for a clean diaper. Embarrassed, I wiped my cheek quickly hoping that the foster mother had not seen, but she had.

"You have to watch these little guys," she admonished with a chuckle, taking the diaper from me to finish the job and handing me a cloth to wipe my face.

The rest of the visit went more smoothly, and I began to feel more confident. No Julie to nibble on my non-existent tie, at least. We discussed Billy's progress, and the foster mother said that she was glad that an adoptive couple was being sought for him. It was far from an inspiring visit, but I felt that it had gone well.

I was less impressed with Jeremy's foster mother. She appeared to have an abundance of children whom she all but ignored as we talked. She was heavy and somewhat slovenly, and her home showed little evidence of attention. Jeremy was not a particularly appealing child, and he sat on the floor and complacently played with his toys. He was not yet walking, despite the fact that he was a year old. The foster mother smoked one cigarette after another and regarded her charges with disinterest. I was secretly glad that Jeremy would be removed from this home soon. The foster mother reported that he had had no further seizures, but the doctor had told her that Jeremy should be placed with a couple who could handle it if he did. He had been tested psychologically and was found to have an I.Q. slightly below average. I wondered if her inattention could have had any effect on this child's apparent lack of interest in his environment. I hoped that placement with an adoptive couple would treat him to a better home life.

If I was discouraged by Jeremy's placement, I was rewarded by Skipper's. Skipper's foster mother, Agnes La Blanc (who insisted that I call her Agnes) was a cheerful, efficient and loving mother whose charges mirrored her positive attention. I fell instantly in love with Skipper, whose deep brown eyes had a twinkle of mischief. He was obviously attached to Agnes, and I wondered how the impending separation would affect them both. Skipper warmed to me easily, perhaps recognizing that he had totally won me over, and Agnes suggested that I take him for a drive to get acquainted. She whispered to me that there was an ice cream place down the block, and that Skipper loved ice cream. Remembering Zach's experience, I opted to sit on a picnic bench while we ate our ice cream. It was unseasonably warm for November, and the sun felt good as we sat there talking. Despite my efforts by eating outside, Skipper's sticky fingers christened my car on the trip back to the foster home. I didn't care, though. I was hooked by this bubbly five-year-old who had an opinion on most subjects, and a question about everything else.

"How come ice cream is sticky," he asked, enjoying how his fingers stuck to my seats.

"Because there is sugar in it, I guess," I answered.

"Is that the stuff that's bad for your teeth? See, this tooth is loose," he said, wiggling the offending tooth. "It's not supposed to be yet, but it is. Are any of your teeth loose?"

I hoped not and told him so, explaining that he would be losing his baby teeth and getting new ones.

"Will you get new ones too?" Again, I hoped not, considering the alternative at my age, but did not think that he needed to know about dentures.

We passed the remainder of the ride back to the foster home in pleasant five-year-old conversation that I found delightful. Some family is in for a real treat, I thought.

Back at the foster home, Skipper scampered into the yard to tell his foster siblings about his ice cream with the social worker, and I talked with Agnes about the plan for finding an adoptive couple for him.

"I hate to have him leave," Agnes admitted, "But we want him to have a family. They have tried to place him before, you know. He was supposed to be placed with his sister, Franny. I don't see why. They don't even know each other. I tried to have them visit, but because Franny lives so far away, it never seemed to work."

"I guess the plan now is to try to place the two children separately," I explained.

"That sounds much more sensible," Agnes agreed. "More coffee?"

I declined and said that I would get back to her when a family had been found. I knew that it would be difficult for this foster mother, but like Mrs. Riley, she was a veteran who wanted the best for the children in her care.

My last call of the day was to Gabby's foster home. Gabby, the three-year-old who had been removed from a severely physically abusive home when she was three months old, had miraculously remained in the same foster home ever since. It would be ideal, on one hand, for children in foster care to remain in one home for as long as this plan was necessary. But the reality was that most children were moved around, whether because of behavior that a particular home could not tolerate, illness, relocation of the foster parents, problems with the foster siblings, or just poor chemistry between family members. There were also those who felt that leaving a child in one foster home until a couple could be found would make the separation from the foster parents more difficult. Although this was certainly true, other critics of the foster care system argued that the stability that a child attained from one placement actually made the future adoptive placement go more smoothly.

Today, there is research being done on attachment and the effects of the attachment disorder that is often a result of multiple moves for children. Attachment is the bonding relationship that we develop with our early caretaker, and the ability to develop this relationship will influence all of our later relations.[1] Children who cannot or have not been given the opportunity to attach successfully are often antisocial, self-absorbed, and have difficulty with intimate relationships. Even now, we have a long way to go before we reform the foster care system in such a manner that children are aided in healthy attachment, but awareness of the issue is the first step.

As I neared Gabby's foster home, I wondered if her sojourn in the Polinskis' foster home would benefit her or inhibit her from attaching to an adoptive couple. I was not looking forward to this visit, as I was the messenger who would have to tell this devoted gram and gramps that they would be losing the child that they had nursed from infancy. When Gabby was removed from her abusive home, the Department attempted to work with her family. The father soon disappeared, and the mother was so inconsistent in her willingness to work for the return of her child that the social worker assigned to Gabby saw little hope for a reunion. In fact, Mom had not even attempted to visit Gabby. Finally convinced that the mother would not be able to care for her child, the social worker pressed for her to sign an adoption surrender, giving up her rights and allowing Gabby to be placed for adoption. Holding on to the last bit of control that she had, Gabby's mom refused to sign the paper, and instead she disappeared from the area and her child's life.

It is difficult to understand how a parent can abandon a child, but over the years, I have begun to recognize that it is not always entirely their choice. The lure of alcohol or drugs, an intimate relationship for a mom who has always felt abandoned in her own life, or a variety of other life circumstances sometimes blur parents' view and convince them that their own needs come before those of their children. In defense of some parents, I must say that some give up their children because they recognize that they are unable to give them the care or nurturing that they deserve. It is easy to judge when you have not been exposed to the situations that bring some folks to separation from their children. But it is important to keep an open mind and occasionally stop and say, "What if I were in his or her shoes?"

No one knew what had caused Gabby's young mother to abandon her. Nevertheless, mom's departure left Gabby in limbo, so the Department filed a petition in probate court for the termination of mom's rights. This petition, after a yearlong standstill in court activity, had just been allowed, and Gabby was now free for adoption. It was this fact that necessitated my visit to the foster home. The foster parents did not yet know that their little girl was up for adoption.

The Polinski foster home was located off of a wooded road with no other houses in close proximity. There were several old cars in the side yard that gave evidence of being worked on, parts strewn across the lawn. An arthritic hound of some unknown breed howled threateningly as I approached. Since he was tied a distance from the front door, and seeing no doorbell, I ventured a knock, undisturbed by his uproar. Another chorus of barking answered my knock, and I could hear someone yell at the

---

[1]For more information, see Levy, T.M., and M. Orlans. 1998. *Attachment, Trauma, and Healing*. Washington, D.C.: Child Welfare League of America.

dogs. Still, no one came to the door. I waited, hearing from beyond the door the unmistakable blare of a television. Okay, I thought. This one will have to be heard over the noise and I brought my knuckles down on the door with more force. The dogs within started to bark again and finally I heard the TV being turned down and footsteps approaching the door. I was immediately bombarded with two small balls of fur that barked much more ferociously than befitted their sizes.

"Tinker! Petey!" a voice that appeared to be connected to a small man behind the dogs had the effect of quieting them. He was shorter than my height of five feet, six inches, by several inches, and after seeing the small dogs, I began to imagine that I had entered a house of munchkins until a very large woman emerged from what appeared to be the sitting room.

"What is it, Herman?"

I heard my cue, and since Herman was looking at me quizzically, I introduced myself.

"Come on in," invited the woman, who I assumed to be Mrs. Polinski. "Gabby's just fine. She's in here." She moved to return to the sitting room. I assumed that I was expected to follow, and smiling at Herman (Mr. Polinski, I guessed) in what I hoped was a reassuring smile, I stepped around the two brown balls of sniffing fur and followed Mrs. Polinski. She led me to an extremely cluttered room, overfilled with furniture and brimming with knickknacks. Her husband followed us, flicked off the television, and went to sit near her. I noticed that she was a good head taller than he and outweighed him by at least a hundred pounds.

"Here she is," Mrs. Polinski said proudly and gestured to an adorable toddler who sat in a high chair eating what must have at one time been a Popsicle®. Now it resembled a small river, most of which was dripping down the child's face and pooling on the tray of the high chair. The child held the stick in her hand and it dripped, but she greeted me with a gooey smile. Her reddish-blonde hair curled around her face, despite being a bit wet in places. She was dressed in a gingham play dress that, before the Popsicle® attack, must have been clean and neat.

"Yes, here's our girl!" Mrs. Polinski lowered her bulk into the chair beside Gabby, wheezing perceptibly and looked lovingly at the child. Gabby giggled in obvious pleasure and gnawed on the now empty stick. The foster mother removed the stick from Gabby's fingers gently, saying, "Now let's get our girl cleaned up for her company. You have a new social worker, honey," she cooed to the child, wiping her hands and face with a ready towel. And then to me, "What did you say your name was, dear?"

I reintroduced myself and sat down in an available chair. I asked how Gabby had been doing, and the foster mother assured me that all was fine, while the silent foster father looked on, seemingly interested and appearing relatively friendly. Tinker and Petey had settled at his feet and must have decided that I was no threat, because they both went to sleep immediately.

"Gabby hasn't had a social worker for a while," said Mrs. Polinski. "Guess we were hoping you'd forgotten about us." She laughed heartily, joined by her husband, but in that laugh I heard something other than mirth.

"In fact," I ventured, wishing above all that I could be anywhere but here and doing anything but delivering this message, "you probably haven't seen anyone because Gabby's social worker left and her case," I immediately regretted calling it that. "The petition on Gabby's behalf has been tied up in court for quite some time. I am sure that the Department felt that you were doing such a good job caring for Gabby that we didn't need to—"

"What petition?" the foster father broke in abruptly. He had a high voice that surprised me, especially compared to his wife's deep contralto.

"The petition to terminate parental rights for the purpose of adoption," I continued weakly, suspecting that I had just treaded on shaky ground.

"Adoption!" echoed the foster mother. "I thought they was going to leave her here. We can take care of her just fine!"

I thought of what I had learned from the foster home record. Both of the foster parents were in their seventies. They had been taking foster children for almost twenty years, but at the moment, Gabby was their only one. The foster father had retired from a furniture factory about ten years ago, and since that time had had three mild heart attacks. He was now on medication for high blood pressure. The foster mother had recently developed emphysema, but maintained that it did not limit her activities in any way. I wondered about this as she seemed to wheeze with every movement. The couple had had one son who was killed while serving in the Army. I was not sure of the exact circumstances, but I did know that they had started taking foster children several years after his death. It did seem obvious, however, that neither one of the foster parents was particularly healthy, and as painful as it might be, Gabby deserved a home that would ensure her care in the future.

As social workers, we are not always content with the choices that we have to make. As I stood watching the looks on Mr. And Mrs. Polinski's faces, I wondered if this was the right career choice for me. We in the field of adoption have also learned a great deal about these tough choices over the years. For the benefit of all, Gabby would probably be placed with a couple that would agree to offer the Polinskis an opportunity to continue as her surrogate grandparents. At that time in history, however, we were not that flexible, and foster and adoptive parents rarely met, much less kept in touch after the adoption placement. As I write about how things were in the 1960s, I cannot believe that we did not recognize the importance of the continuity of the love and stability of caring foster parents to a child.

I forged on, talking to the Polinskis about how a couple would be sought for Gabby, and how she would be presented to them first on paper and then in person. A series of visits would follow, culminating in an overnight stay and then the final placement. I watched helplessly as my words seemed to drive daggers further into these parents' hearts, but I was inexperienced and knew of no other way to do my job. I rationalized that the Polinskis must have been told before that the plan for Gabby was eventual adoption, but the point seemed moot right then.

Having dropped my bomb and noticing a perceptible change in the couple's affect toward me, I decided it was time to leave. I fantasized that even Tinker and Petey were looking at me with hatred and plotting a more effective strategy of attack when I returned. As I drove home, I wished that this visit had not been my last. I felt deflated and discouraged, and needed some words of encouragement. But the office would be closed and I didn't want to bother Herb at home, even if I knew where he lived. I went home, glad that my folks would be there and hoping that they would understand how rotten I was feeling.

Questions for Thought

1. How would you feel if you did not hit it off with a particular foster mother, or if you did not like her style of parenting? What would you do?

2. Evaluating a child's development is part textbook learning and part intuition. How would you feel about evaluating a child's development and readiness for adoption?

3. How do you think foster parents feel when a child that they have cared for is about to leave? Can you identify the emotions that they might experience?

4. How do you feel about parents who abandon their children? What might be some of the causes? How might you relate to them?

5. How might you have handled the visit with the Polinskis? What would your initial impressions have been?

6. What thought do you think might have been going on in the Polinskis' minds? How might you have helped them?

6

In Search of the Perfect Parents

The next Monday morning found me once again in Herb's office, getting a lesson on how to find adoptive homes for the children I had seen.

"Each couple is coded according to what they are looking for in a child," explained my supervisor. "The homefinder, a worker who does their homestudy, has assessed not only their interest in children, but also their ability to accept a variety of different issues. For example, let's say that a couple is hoping for a Caucasian, preferably Northern European, boy between the ages of zero and two years old."

He jotted down these facts and spouted off several others. To me, it felt like ordering through a catalogue that tells you to specify the exact size, color and style. But Herb assured me that the current research indicated that the adoption experience would go much more smoothly if the couple's preferences were taken into consideration.

"Once the couple has been approved for adoption, their name, along with all their preferences, is placed in this card-sort box. Enter the placement worker, you!" Herb smiled at me with encouragement as I tried to take it all in. "You have a child with specific characteristics, and you need to find a couple that will match. Let's take Billy, for example. That one should be easy. Three month old Caucasian boy, healthy and ready to go." He deftly stuck a metal rod similar to a knitting needle into the front card in the box that listed the characteristic "male." Several other needles were also inserted into other identifying characteristics. With skill, Herb shook out the remainder of the cards that had not been caught up by the group of needles.

"There you go," he chuckled. "The perfect match for Billy!"

"But there must be thirty cards there!" I protested.

"Looks like you have your morning cut out for you looking over these files. You might start with those couples that have been approved the longest. No point in keeping people waiting any longer than necessary."

When I think how we accomplished this matching in those days compared to the computer matching of today, the old ways seem truly archaic. We now try to help adoptive applicants become more flexible in what they can accept as well. Our concept of matching has changed considerably. Paradoxically, when matching is so much easier by computer, the homefinder—sometimes called the family resource worker or a variety of other names depending upon the agency—has taken on increasing importance. Often, the placement worker goes directly to his/her homefinding counterpart to get ideas of which couples to research. Homefinders often know the couples they have studied well, and can make assessments based on information that might not have been reflected in the record.

Noticing that I was overwhelmed by the number of couples who could be potential families for Billy, Herb assured me that the matching did not always yield so many options.

"For some kids, you find no matches," he explained.

"What happens then?" I asked.

"There are several possibilities. Sometimes the homefinders know of a couple that can stretch a bit. For example, a couple that wants a baby might be willing to take a sibling group but had never thought of it. The other alternative is to search the Adoption Resource Exchange catalogues," he said, hefting a large spiral binder onto the desk.

"What's that?" I asked, imaging another magnitude of paperwork that I would have to peruse.

"The Exchanges are both statewide and national. This is the book for ARENA, the Adoption Resource Exchange of America. This lists both couples and children from across the USA. There is one for Massachusetts called MARE."

I flipped tentatively through the book he offered me, seeing pictures of smiling children along with descriptions of them. In another section, equally expectant couples stared from the pages, willing me to find the right child for them.

"These are organized according to characteristics as well. You might look in here for a family for Skipper. We haven't had any luck finding anyone around here." Herb went on to explain that in conservative Boston, where at the time a mixed-race child was considered by some couples to be a child who was part Irish and part Italian, the idea of a child whose parentage was half Hispanic might be more of a challenge to place.

"We presented Skipper to a couple verbally before," Herb said, "but they thought he looked too Hispanic. They mentioned his very broad nose and black eyes."

I was shocked by this admission. Those were some of the features that made Skipper so appealing. If only they had met him, I thought.

"In fact," Herb continued, "it is tougher to place a child who is part Hispanic than one who is half Black."

As I recall this, I marvel at how the adoption field has changed. Children are now accepted more because they are children than for their racial background. With the increasing Hispanic population, there would be no difficulty whatsoever in placing Skipper today.

Armed with my newfound knowledge, I spent the better part of the day finding parents for my four children, Billy, Gabby, Jeremy, and Skipper. I was stuck on Skipper, having leafed through both the ARENA and MARE books for some time, when another worker approached me. I had asked several of the homefinders questions as I was reading several couples' folders, and Jill, a tall attractive homefinder, asked what progress I had made. When I told her that I was still searching for a home for Skipper, she thought for a minute.

"I just got an update packet from ARENA and I haven't even looked at it yet. Let's take a look." She pulled the manila envelope open and spread the pages that would soon be added to the ARENA book across her desk.

"Hey, how about these folks!" she said excitedly as she studied one sheet with the experienced eye of a veteran homefinder. "They look perfect."

The Van Dykes, Laura, Joe, Megan, and Sarah smiled up at me with an air of confidence. Joe was a professor of history at a midwestern college, and his wife Laura was a part-time travel agent. The write-up explained that their daughters, Megan, 14 years old, and Sarah, 12 years old, were dying for a little brother. They were willing to take a child from any racial background and cared only that he was younger than their two girls.

"With that flexibility, why haven't they been snatched up?" I wondered out loud.

Jill looked at the name of the agency on the bottom of the sheet and answered, "This is a small agency in a somewhat remote area. My guess is that they just finished their home study and have been approved. The agency probably doesn't have too many children and registered them with ARENA so there would be more choices for them. I would suggest that you call the clearinghouse right away and get the complete record. A couple like this will probably be in high demand."

By the time I left that day, I had contacted an ARENA representative and discussed the Van Dykes in more detail. I had also arranged to have a copy of their record sent to me by overnight mail. Already I was convinced that they were the family for Skipper. Herb suggested that I make contact with the couple as soon as I had seen the file, and I left feeling that I had accomplished a great deal. How different from my day in the field!

On Tuesday I was filled with excitement. I quickly made a list of what I needed to do:

1) For Gabby—Call the Devers, a couple with a 7-year-old son.
2) For Skipper—Wait for the file on the Van Dykes. Read it over and call them if it looked good.
3) For Jeremy—Call the Ragusas, a couple with no children.
4) For Billy—Decide between the two couples that I had files for. Both seemed appropriate.

My first call to an adoptive couple had me especially nervous. Since the Devers were first on my list, I tried them first. I had rehearsed my speech carefully. I would say who I was, where I was from, and that I thought we had a child from them. Then I would arrange to have them come to the office, so that I might share with them a description and pictures of the child. After going over what I was to say, I was disappointed that the Devers did not answer. Before the days when almost everyone had an answering machine, I had no way of leaving a message, and could only hope that they would be home later. On to the Ragusas.

The phone rang twice and a throaty female voice said, "Hello?" I took a deep breath and began my pitch, trying to sound friendly and encouraging. But no sooner had I finished saying who I was and where I was from when the woman's voice burst with an excited cry of, "Mama Mia! Mary and Joseph be praised! It's them, Mario! It's my bambino!" A flood of Italian to someone in the background made it impossible for me to continue.

A male voice came on the line. "I'm sorry," he said. "Is this really the adoption people?" I assured him that it was and got out a bit more of my speech. He explained in an excited voice, "My wife is overcome. You will have to forgive her, but she has looked forward to this call for so long. I am so glad I had today off. Sure, we will come. When? Today? We can be there in an hour!"

I had certainly not expected to see the couple that day, but I was enveloped by their enthusiasm. I agreed that I would be glad to meet with them in the office at 4:00. Once off the phone, I sought out Herb, trying to keep my composure but having no idea what I would say when the couple arrived. He laughed at my experience and suggested that I take Jeremy's picture from the record and jot down some pertinent facts about him to share with the couple.

"From the initial reception you got," he mused, "I doubt that this will be a tough one. Maybe the hard part will be getting a word in!"

To calm my nerves, I spent the next half hour rereading the two files I had chosen for Billy. Still uncertain, I noticed that they were both studied by the same home-finder, Everett Marsh. I sought out his advice.

"I'd suggest you use the O'Donnells," he told me. "They have been waiting for a while." I was not impressed by his lack of enthusiasm but I decided that I would take his advice. Still unable to reach the Devers, I called the O'Donnells. They were another childless couple, and I wondered if I would get the same type of excitement that the Ragusas demonstrated. But the voice that answered the phone, Mrs. O'Donnell, I assumed, was quiet and unperturbed by my news. Since their home was a two hour drive from the Central office, I scheduled to see them in a smaller area office closer to their home several days later. Mrs. O'Donnell said that her husband was on the road but would be back the next day. We agreed that our interview would take place on Friday, allowing Mr. O'Donnell to have a couple of days at home. She had asked nothing about the baby and I could only describe my feeling as lukewarm. Then I decided that any reaction after Mrs. Ragusa's would have been a distinct contrast.

When I returned from lunch, I tried once again to call the Devers and was rewarded by an answer. Mrs. Dever was a pleasant woman whose voice expressed the enthusiasm that Mrs. O'Donnell's had lacked, albeit with more restraint than Mrs. Ragusa. I liked her immediately when she asked all about Gabby and it sounded like my answers were just what she had hoped for. She said that they would love to come in but she would have to get in touch with her husband who, as a store manager, was in the busy season of the year. We agreed that she would get back to me and I hung up.

"Guess what I have!" said Herb, who held out a large envelope that had just arrived.

"The Van Dykes?"

He nodded and I eagerly grabbed the package, ripping it open. The picture was the first piece that caught my eye. The one in the ARENA book had been small, black and white, and poorly reproduced, but this one, in color, showed the family in more detail. There was Laura Van Dyke, blonde and fair, but with the darkest eyes I had ever seen on a blonde. Her face was square with its most prominent feature being a broad flat nose. I laughed in recognition. She was a blonde Skipper!

"This is it!" I assured Herb, even before reading the file.

"Well aren't you the confident one all of a sudden. Just for that, I'll give you another case that just came in!" he said, good-naturedly handing me another file.

"Ugh," I groaned. "I was feeling like I had everything under control!"

"Well, we can't have that," he joked. "Maybe I can scare up another case before the day is over."

This would be the first and only time during my years in both adoption and protective services that I would feel like I was ahead of my cases. Today, workers in most states should only be handling between fifteen and twenty cases at any given time. While I worked at the adoption unit, my caseload number rose to forty. Granted, they were not all active at the same time. Some cases required only an infrequent visit while we waited for the legally required supervisory year to pass. Even in my protective caseload in later years, my case count was at one time as much as eighty. Fortunately, some of those required little attention, but to know that one is responsible for eighty cases is a great responsibility. It is not surprising that caseloads have been drastically reduced. Yet, any caseworker will tell you that even twenty families can take a great deal of time.

My call to the Van Dykes was one that I anticipated with some trepidation. Despite my initial enthusiasm, I had begun to have doubts. What if they were not right for Skipper, to whom I had become overly attached in just one visit? How would I know at such a distance? They had been studied by a homefinder in another agency, and I would not even meet them unless I was the one to transport Skipper. This was the life of a very special child that I was orchestrating. Did I have the skill or knowledge to do it in his best interest? Unsure, I dropped by Herb's office and shared my fears with him.

"That's the tough part of this job," he sympathized. "Wondering if you've done the best thing. But your gut reaction was positive, so you just have to have faith that it's the right placement. We're not gods. We make mistakes. Sometimes we just have to go on faith." He was very serious as he said this last bit, and I realized that there was more to Herb than the affable man I had known for only a week. He took his job very seriously, and I wanted to be that kind of a worker, too. But he was right. I had to go on faith.

I reviewed the Van Dykes' file and picked up the phone. A deep baritone answered.

"Dr. Van Dyke?"

"Yes?" he replied, tentative but friendly.

He greeted my pronouncement of a possible child for them with warm enthusiasm. As we spoke, I suddenly realized that I had no idea how out-of-state adoptions were handled. Did the couple come here? Did we do everything over the phone? How was the other agency involved? Fortunately, the potential adoptive father was better prepared than I was.

"I know we are supposed to come out to meet with you," he began. "And Laura will shoot me for this, but we are right in the middle of mid-semester exams. I could get time off in two weeks. Would that be okay?"

Surprised that they would fly all the way out here to meet Skipper and unsure of what I was supposed to say, I stumbled, "Well, yes, I guess but . . ."

Perhaps assuming that my hesitation was an admonishment of his not wanting to jump on a plane immediately, Dr. Van Dyke interrupted, "Could we hear about him anyway, Laura and I? She's working right now, but she will be home in a couple of hours. We could call you, or you could get back to us." His rapid-fire speech was something to which I would become accustomed. An academic all the way, he thought as fast as he spoke, if not faster, and was a definite contrast, I would learn, to his thoughtful, deliberate wife. We set a time for the next day when we would have a conference call, so that I could tell him and his wife about the child I hoped they would want to adopt.

When I returned to my desk from the group phone (three or four workers were assigned to one phone since it was rare that all were in the office on the same day), I discovered that Herb had made good on his threat to give me more cases. Two new files sat on my desk in addition to the one he had handed me earlier that day. Back to work! But a quick look at my watch told me that it was almost four and I had best collect my thoughts and materials so that I could present Jeremy to the Ragusas.

As I started for the lobby to see if my clients had arrived, I was flagged by Gertie, one of the secretaries.

"Do you have Fontaine?" she asked urgently. Fortunately, I recognized the name as one of the new files that Herb had just given me. When I nodded, she pointed to a nearby phone. "Call for you on line two." Grimacing, she returned to her work.

"This is Attorney Gaven," said the voice on the other end of the line. "I represent Dolores Fontaine, the mother of Celestine and Kevin. Your Department has filed a petition to terminate my client's parental rights. I just wanted to let you know that my client will appear at the hearing next Thursday and we will fight this outrage."

I was speechless. I had not had a chance to read the file, nor did I know anything about an "outrage." Stuttering in the face of this hostile pronouncement, I explained that I had just gotten the file and had not had a chance to read it. That apparently was not the correct response, as I was treated to a barrage of complaints about the inefficiency of the agency and how we targeted poor and loving parents and tried to snatch their children. The tirade was followed by a distinct "click," leaving me shaken and unsure. Zach, who happened to be heading for the lobby as well, saw my face.

"What's up, kid?" he quipped, trying to lighten the mood.

"An Attorney Gaven . . ." I began.

"Oh, Gaven! Don't worry about it! He targets the new workers. He thinks he can bully them. Just know your case when you go in and you'll be fine."

Still unconvinced and making a note to read the file immediately and run this by Herb, I accompanied Zach to greet my clients. Unfortunately, the call from Attorney Gaven had not made me feel especially competent, but I shouldn't have worried. The Ragusas could not stop talking and made it very easy for me to relax.

Theresa Ragusa greeted me first with a big smile. She was a large woman with a round, pleasant face and abundant black curls. Her red outfit accentuated her coloring. Was it my imagination that she smelled faintly of spaghetti sauce? I could picture her ample frame smiling over a simmering pot of pasta and encouraging her guests to "Eat! Eat!" She exuded warmth and love. Mario, her husband, was equally robust but more quiet.

"So what kind of bambino do you have for us, little lady?" bubbled Theresa Ragusa, in a voice tinged with the faintest hint of an Italian accent. Knowing that they were from a predominantly Italian community, this was not surprising.

"A boy?" asked her husband. They had specified either gender but were thrilled that I had told them on the phone that it was a boy.

I extracted the pictures of Jeremy from the folder I had prepared and Theresa immediately began her chant again.

"Mama Mia! He is beautiful! Mary and Joseph be praised, what a beautiful baby!"

"It's been a long time that we've waited," explained Mario, as if in defense of his wife. "We both have big families and my Theresa has watched one family member after another have babies. She so wants to be a mother!"

It was obvious as his wife cooed over the pictures as if they were the real thing. I saw Jeremy as somewhat colorless compared to the adorable Gabby or Billy, but this couple had found beauty in this child's face and I was glad for them. I only hoped that quiet Jeremy could endure what would surely be an onslaught of affection.

"What's next?" asked Mario Ragusa over his wife's continued appreciative exclamations.

I explained carefully about the seizure that Jeremy had had and that there was always the possibility of another.

"That's not a problem," chimed in Theresa. "My sister Mary's son had those. He outgrew them." She would not be deterred.

I explained that he tested slightly below average and was a bit developmentally behind, but medical testing had not indicated any retardation.

"That would be okay too," Theresa added. "My cousin Margaret's baby is retarded, but she's the sweetest little girl. Just a bundle of love."

I was secretly glad that Mrs. Ragusa could not be discouraged and had renewed confidence in Jeremy's future.

Mr. Ragusa began to explain to me that they had child care arranged. Theresa was at home, but if she needed to get out, he could take the baby with him to the barber shop.

"My cousin Al works with me and he brings his kids down, too. When they were little, they had this little walker thing that they buzzed around in."

"I'll be home!" Theresa insisted firmly. Seeing the disappointment on her husband's face, she added, "But I'll bring the bambino in to see you, dear." He brightened.

I thought that it was best that we arrange how the "bambino" would meet his new parents, so I explained how they would see him in a neutral place and if all went well, I would bring him to their home the next day.

"Why can't we have him the day that we meet him?" asked the anxious mother-to-be.

Good question, I thought to myself, and then I remembered something Herb had said about giving the couple an opportunity to have any second thoughts and also to prepare. Why was it that I doubted that Theresa and Mario Ragusa would have second thoughts? As I explained that this was policy, I made a mental note to talk to Herb about the possibility of making the actual placement later that day. With this in mind, I scheduled the Ragusas' meeting with Jeremy for Thursday morning, giving them a full day to prepare. I was exhausted when the Ragusas left, but feeling elated that my first initial placement interview had gone so well.

Questions for Thought

1. The matching of children and parents has changed considerably over the years. How much matching do you feel is necessary between adoptive parents and children, and why?

2. Certainly, the computer makes matching much easier today. What might be some of the disadvantages of using the computer to match adoptive parents and children?

3. What might be the advantages and the disadvantages of an adoption exchange? Does one outweigh the other?

4. How might you have reacted had you been the one to call Mrs. Ragusa? What would your impression of her have been?

5. How would it affect you if you had a job that you never could keep entirely ahead of? How would you react in such a situation?

6. How would it make you feel to pick out couples for children? What fears might you have? How would you resolve these?

7. How might you have responded to Attorney Gavin? How would he have made you feel?

7

Getting My Teeth into It

When I arrived for work on Wednesday morning, my head was full of all that I expected to do in the next few days. I nodded absent-mindedly to Gertie, the secretary, who happened to be the only one taking the elevator with me at that time. She said nothing , but I hardly noticed, I was so engrossed in my thoughts. When she began to mutter, I looked around to see that we were indeed the only occupants of the elevator. But she was not addressing her words to me and I returned to my thoughts, assuming that she was talking to herself. I was not above the practice when I had something on my mind.

The last couple of days had been devoted to getting to know my new cases. In addition to the court case that was scheduled on Thursday, there were two others. One was Barton, a case that would soon be heard in probate court, and the other, Hunter, a relatively straightforward case involving an infant that had just been released for adoption by her young, unwed mother. As I read over Jessica Barton's case, I was puzzled by a significant number of blank spaces in the dictation. I gleaned that three-year-old Jessica had been sexually abused by mother's boyfriend and had been removed from her mother's home because Mom continued to endanger her by not asking the boyfriend to leave. Then there was an entry that suggested that Mom had actually helped in the abuse. It was difficult to imagine how a mother could have done such a thing, but I remembered Herb saying that we could not pass judgment unless we have walked in another's shoes. Apparently the Juvenile Court had agreed with me, because they had given the Department custody of little Jessica. Now it was up to the Adoption Unit to secure a petition from Probate Court so that we might place her for adoption. The petition, I noticed, had been filed some time ago, and would be coming up in several weeks. I made a note to talk to Herb about this case in my supervision meeting that afternoon.

Tara Hunter was a four-month-old Black baby whose unwed mother, a high school senior, had finally been able to release her for adoption. I noticed that there was also an adoption surrender from the father, and imagined that this must have been a difficult choice for these two young people. When a couple is unmarried, the father technically has no rights to the child. In recent years, biological fathers have fought for the right to raise their children. Thus, many social workers sought an adoption surrender from a biological father if he showed the slightest bit of interest in the child he had helped to produce.

I was looking forward to my first official supervision meeting with Herb. When 10:00 rolled around, the time appointed for our meeting, I had so many questions and was eager to get more deeply into my cases. With his ever-present cup of coffee, Herb greeted me warmly as I entered his office.

"How's it going?"

I assured him that all was well and immediately launched into my cases.

"You are the eager beaver!" he quipped, as I fired my questions at him.

When I asked why there were so many blanks in the dictation of Jessica Barton's file, he laughed.

"That, my dear, is a valuable lesson in the joys of civil service."

Puzzled, I awaited his further explanation.

"Remember how I once told you to try to avoid giving the files to Gertie to type?" He began closing the door of his office so that his words would remain between us.

"Yes, but what does that . . ."

"Well, Gertie has a little problem . . . well several actually but in this case . . . She feels that the graphic explanation of sexual deviations is sinful and that we will all go to hell. Therefore, she refuses to type any of these words into the file. This necessitates that every time we go to court, we all sit around like a group of perverts, trying to figure out which sexual words should have gone into which blanks."

"I don't believe it!" I exclaimed. "Has anyone spoken to her?"

"Oh, yes! Many times. She always agrees to change, but the next file she types, it's the same thing."

"Why don't they fire her?" I asked.

"That is where civil service comes in. She is a civil service employee and they cannot be fired. Their jobs are guaranteed!"

I was to learn much about the civil service system in my years of working for the State. I would see competent workers let go because someone else had scored higher on a civil service exam for that position. I would see incompetent people who could not be fired because they had civil service standing. Fortunately, there have been many changes, and today, someone like Gertie would probably not be allowed to remain in her position.

As I thought over the problems that Gertie created, Herb continued.

"Don't be alarmed, though. She's harmless. We think that she is mentally ill and is supposed to be on medication. It's a bit unnerving when you think she's talking to you and she's engaged in her own self-absorbed world. That happened to me one time in the elevator."

"So that's what that was about." I described my morning's ride with the secretary.

"She's a good person," he finished. "But she is a bit different."

I thought that that was a bit understated, but said nothing. Herb assured me that we would take time to try to fill in the missing words from the Barton file before I went to court. I filled Herb in on my other cases as well. I had had a conference call with the Van Dykes and they very much wanted to go ahead with their meeting with Skipper. They felt that they could come to Massachusetts next week when I could arrange a meeting between them and the child. Herb was encouraging, and said that I had done well with that case so far. I explained that I had also set up a meeting with the Devers next week, and after I presented Gabby to them, I would be arranging a meeting. I would also be seeing the O'Donnells. We concluded our meeting with Herb's praise of my impending placements and his explanation of how the logistics of each should work. He admonished me to pace myself, lest I burn myself out too soon. Little did I know how wise his advice would be.

On Thursday I presented Jeremy to the Ragusas, who swept the somewhat startled child into their arms as he and I arrived to meet them at a restaurant close to their home. The baby took it well, and they actually had him smiling by the end of the visit. They both proclaimed that he was the most adorable baby they had ever seen. As I suspected, they had no doubts about this being the child for them. I had gotten pre-approval from Herb to bring the baby to them later that day, and had already prepared the foster mother for that possibility. Not surprisingly, she expressed no objections. So it was that Jeremy was soon to become Mario Jeremiah (Jerry for short) in the home of Theresa and Mario Ragusa.

It was the practice of the Department to follow the protocol I had used with the Ragusas for any baby under a year. Older children often required several visits and more careful observation of their reactions. Since Jeremy was just a year old and was not particularly bonded to his foster home, Herb felt that the infant protocol would suffice. It was also the practice at that time to verbally prepare older children for the placement, while it was assumed that infants had little comprehension. But I was convinced that babies understood long before we gave them credit for doing so, so I babbled to Jeremy as we returned to the foster home. I have no idea how much he understood, but he didn't cry, so I assumed that he was listening.

Before I returned Jeremy to his expectant adoptive parents, I had a less enviable task. At 11:00, I was to appear in Probate Court on the matter of a petition to terminate the rights of Dolores Fontaine so that her children, Celestine and Kevin, might be released for adoption. Herb had described it as a sticky case and had apologized for giving it to me when I was so inexperienced. He promised me that Denise, the protective services social worker, would also be there. She was an experienced worker, and Herb assured me that I was in good company. It was up to me only to testify to the importance of adoption for these children, while Denise, who had worked with their mother, knew more about why they were no longer with Miss Fontaine.

Mentally, I reviewed what I had read about the case. Dolores Fontaine had become pregnant with Celestine when she was seventeen. The child's father was unknown. Dolores had been an alcoholic since she was fifteen, and had also done a few drugs. Miraculously, Celestine was unaffected by her mother's substance abuse. A year later, Dolores had become pregnant with Kevin. This baby was drug addicted at birth, but was returned to the mother at three months when she promised that she would no longer abuse drugs. With two babies under two years old, the twenty-year-old mother took up with another man who physically abused both children. Dolores left him, but soon reverted to her drug abuse. When Kevin was four, Dolores brought him to a friend and left him, saying that she could no longer handle him. The friend insisted that she also leave Celestine, who was then five and a half. The children were so badly scarred, dehydrated, and malnourished that the friend called the Department and placed the children in their care. A petition was filed in Juvenile Court alleging abuse and neglect by the mother. A weeping Dolores appeared at court, promising that she would never again neglect or harm her children, but the judge was not convinced. He gave legal custody of both children to the Department and they were placed in foster care. They were placed in different foster homes as the friend observed that even at four, Kevin was extremely abusive to his sister, perhaps mirroring what he had seen at home. Once denied her children, Dolores refused to work with social workers and seemed to drop from sight.

At six, Kevin was so disturbed that he was placed in a residential setting for aggressive children, while Celestine (called Tina by the foster parents) settled comfortably as the only child in a loving foster home for the duration of her stay in foster care. Numerous attempts had been made to find Dolores, but to no avail. Now the children were eight and nine, and it seemed that their futures must be decided. Tina's devoted foster parents were moving out of state and had asked to take her with them. This would not be possible unless they could adopt her. In the meantime, the residential setting that had treated Kevin for the last two years felt that he was ready to be placed in a home, and sought his release from their center. The social worker had filed the petition for termination of Dolores' rights, so that her children could get on with their lives.

When such a petition is filed, it is legally necessary to publish a notification in the newspaper serving the parent's last known residence. So it was that someone had notified Dolores, now living in West Virginia, that her children were about to be released for adoption. The call from Attorney Gavin heralded her return, and it was clear that the court hearing would not be a simple half hour formality, but a heated court battle. It was now up to Dolores to prove that her children should not be placed for adoption.

The old courthouse was hot and stuffy as we waited for the hearing to commence. Denise Foreman, the protective social worker who had handled the Fontaine case since it was opened, was a short woman whose deep brown complexion was complemented by a bright pink suit. She was friendly and open, and assured me that there was no way that the judge would agree to give Dolores another chance.

"Honey, if you had seen these kids when they came into care! Oowie! They were a mess. All scars and blisters and their little bellies were just crying for a good meal. No mother can change that much!" Her confidence eased my anxiety, and I looked forward to seeing justice at its best. I quickly lost some of my confidence, however, when Denise did a bit of a double take as Dolores entered the courtroom. The mother was a tall blonde, whose slender figure was clothed in a stunning emerald green dress. Her nails were long, polished, and elegant, and she looked as if she had just stepped out of a women's magazine featuring an article on "How to Make the Most of What You Have."

"Whew," breathed Denise under her breath. "Has that lady gone and changed!"

Then she smiled and added, "But motherhood is more than looking good, honey. She's going to have to prove she can be a mom too."

But prove Dolores Fontaine did, or at least her lawyer did. I had to admit that Attorney Gavin was good, and by the time the day was over, he could have convinced even me, had I not read the record, that Dolores had been a wonderful mother to her children. The Department, on the other hand, was presented by Mr. Gavin as the bad guys who came between a mother and her children.

"Well, you have seen the justice system at its best," said Denise Foreman as we gathered our files to leave the courtroom. The case had been continued until the next day, but my coworker did not seem hopeful.

"But the judge has seen our records," I argued. "He must realize that she was abusive and neglectful to these children. How could he not want them adopted by a loving family?"

"Come on, let's get some coffee. I need to unwind," Denise told me. I suspected that she also wanted the privacy that the courtroom did not allow us. We found a nearby coffee shop, and over my soda and her coffee, she answered my concerns.

"Sure, he saw the records, but that was years ago that she had them. She presents a great picture now. And you heard Gavin. The lady's turned over a new leaf."

"What happens to the children if the judge denies our petition?" I asked.

"Ah, now there's the rub," Denise began flagging the waitress for a refill. "If the petition to terminate Mom's rights is denied, the Department still has legal custody. But for what? We can't allow Tina's nice foster family to take her away, so she would have to go to another foster home. And what happens to Kevin now that he is ready to be released from residential treatment? Ditto. We have to find another foster home." She paused while the waitress refilled her cup and bustled off to answer another customer's bidding.

"So what's best for these kids? You can bet that if Mom wins this ballgame, she will go on with Mr. Smart Lawyer to appeal our custody. And then there will be more court battles and the kids get bounced around. No, I think that if we lose, the Department will have to return the kids to Mom." Denise threw down several bills and said with a smile, "My treat. Part of the first lesson in the injustice of justice."

"But what if she can't be a good parent?" I wasn't willing to let it drop.

"Well, honey," Denise began, "we just better hope that Ms. Foreman is as good at improving her mothering as she is at transforming her looks."

I glanced at my watch and realized that I still had to deliver Jeremy to his adoptive home.

"Oh gosh! I'm late! Thanks for the coffee and I'm sorry to run! See you tomorrow!"

"No problem, honey," Denise said in parting. "Good luck with the placement! Wish I had happy jobs!"

I was relieved that my day would end on a positive note. The foster mother had Jeremy fully packed when I arrived, admittedly a bit late. She didn't seem terribly upset about his leaving, and I was thankful that I was transporting the baby to a home where I had no doubt that he would be the center of attention.

I arrived at the Ragusas' home to discover almost no place to park. The driveway was full, as was the street surrounding their home. I was trying to decide on the best plan that did not involve carrying a baby and all his belongings from a block away when Mario Ragusa came running out to my car.

"We're so sorry!" he apologized hastily, "I know that you suggested that we be alone when you brought the baby. But you were a bit late, and our family was so anxious to meet him."

I met his apology with my own for being held up at court (or in actuality, at coffee processing the events of court), and he promised to clear a parking spot for me. Within minutes, there was a flurry of departing cars, though I had no doubt that they would be back soon after I left. Mario returned to help me with the baby and his gear.

"I hope it's okay, but our mothers are still here," he said guiltily. "My father-in-law left, but I just couldn't kick out my mother or Terry's. Is it okay?"

What could I say? If it worked for the family, I guessed it was okay with me. Mario took Jeremy gently, as if he was a fragile object, and I tagged along feeling like the porter. Predictably, Mrs. Ragusa's cries of enthusiasm were joined by two more, and I wondered if Jeremy was having second thoughts. But he looked happy enough as three doting women helped him out of his coat. We talked for a bit more, and I gave the Ragusas the schedule I had asked the foster mother to write out. Both grandmothers assured me that they would "help Theresa get the knack of mothering," and I was sure that there would be no lack of suggestions from them. I told Theresa and Mario that I would call the next day to see how they were getting along, and for the next year I would be making visits about every three months or so. Between visits, they were welcome to call me with questions. I left feeling elated and confident that, despite the confusion, Jeremy would settle in with little trouble. How could one be that much loved and not enjoy it?

Despite the happy ending to my day, I spent a somewhat sleepless night thinking about Tina and Kevin. I had met Tina's foster parents and had liked them a great deal. Tina seemed so happy with them, and I could not see her uprooted. Although I had only seen Kevin briefly, I had talked with his residential social worker, who felt that he had made excellent progress. I hoped that this progress would not be jeopardized.

No one was surprised when the judge banged down his gavel the next day with the pronouncement: petition denied. It was not long before Attorney Gavin approached Denise and me with the information that his client would like to meet with Denise, the worker on the case, as soon as possible. My involvement in the case had ended when all possibility of adoption had been denied by the court. Now it was up to Denise and her office, who specialized in protective services, to deal with the case.

I was tired and drained as I headed back to the office. I could only hope that a new Dolores Fontaine would now make good her promise to be a better mother to her two children. I also thought sadly of Tina's foster parents, who had parented an abused and neglected child into health and would probably lose her to an uncertain future. It had been an enlightening two days, and I was quickly learning that situations in social work practice did not always turn out as I hoped. I turned my thoughts to the more hopeful aspects of my work, and anticipated meeting with the potential adoptive parents of Billy, Gabby, and Skipper.

Questions for Thought

1. How might you have responded to Gertie? What might you have said to her?

2. How do you feel about Jessica Barton's parents? Would it have influenced your ability to work with the child?

3. What do you think should have been done about Gertie, understanding that, due to civil service regulations, she could not be fired? How would you deal with her?

4. What are your impressions of Dolores Fontaine? How might you have worked with her?

5. How would you have reacted to a court hearing such as the Fontaines'? What would you have done in Denise Foreman's place?

6. How might you have handled the Ragusa placement? How did this placement make you feel?

8

A Week of Introductions

I was excited about meeting with the O'Donnells on Friday. Buoyed by the positive experience I had had with the Ragusas, I was looking forward to another joyful adoptive placement. Both Herb and Zach had assured me that just because I was not ecstatic about Mrs. O'Donnell over the phone, that did not mean a thing. In person, she might be totally different, and furthermore, another worker told me kindly, this was not a popularity contest. Just because a couple was not my favorite, it did not mean that they would not be good parents.

I was greeted by a bevy of excited workers who thrust a card and a pen in my face and urged me to sign. It seemed that it was another supervisor's birthday, and they were circulating a card to be signed. The contingent of planners hoped that I would be available at 3:00, when they were going to have a cake for her. One of the best memories I have about the social work offices, especially later when I did protective services work, was the camaraderie. If we worked hard and dealt with difficult clients, we needed to play hard as well. The offices where morale is high are the most effective. I assured everyone that I would try to be there, and set off for my desk, only to be intercepted once again by Deirdre, one of the other workers in my unit. She told me that Herb had scheduled a unit meeting since all his supervisees were supposed to be in that day. Unit meetings were to become one of the more rewarding parts of my work in the adoption unit. Having the opportunity to share successes and failures with my colleagues helped me to recognize that I was on track. It was always fun to get a renewed taste of Zach's humor as we sat around and compared notes. Unfortunately, not all supervisors had such meetings, and when I was later to leave Herb's supervision, I would miss them.

This day, I learned that Zach's little Julie had been placed with a couple and appeared to be doing well. Jason, the child who had christened Zach's new car, had had a bit of trouble acclimating to his new foster home at first, but now seemed to be doing well. I also learned that I had more pending placements scheduled than any of my coworkers, which made my competitive side feel good. Then I remembered

Herb's suggestions about pacing myself. But I loved the work, and enjoyed the idea of families finally having the children they had hoped for.

Deirdre, Scott, Zach, and Samantha all discussed their cases, and they listened as I recounted the frustrating moments in court with the Fontaine case. The newer workers were as incredulous as I had been about the possible outcome, now that the petition to terminate Dolores' rights had been denied. Deirdre had a contested case coming up in a few weeks, and we wished her luck that it was not similar.

"It has got to be really hard for some of these foster parents to lose the kids when we place them," Samantha piped in as we moved on to other topics.

"It is," said Herb. "You might want to check in with them the next day or so after placement to see how they are doing." This was something that had not occurred to me. I doubted that Jeremy's foster mother had been devastated by his leaving, but I could imagine the Polinskis when Gabby finally left. I was sure, too, that Mrs. Reilly, Julie's former foster mother, would appreciate a call from Zach to tell her that Julie was doing well.

"I thought that foster parents were part of the team," Scott's voice interrupted my thoughts.

"They are," said Herb. "But parenting a child twenty-four hours a day and seven days a week is also an emotional commitment. For some of our foster parents, this is their lives."

"Funny, you sometimes hear that foster parents are just in it for the money," added Deirdre. "But it sure doesn't seem that way to me."

"Sure, there might be an occasional foster parent who takes in a lot of kids and is pretty well paid. Maybe you could say that it's for the money. But the money isn't great, and the responsibilities are a lot greater. Most of these folks have to be really interested in kids to want to be foster parents," explained Herb.

I was to meet many loving and competent foster parents in my years in both adoption and protective services. I also learned that a social worker could better serve a child by working closely with his or her foster parents.

Our unit meeting concluded with Herb's reminder that we must be sure to complete the paperwork and do our dictations after each case meeting. He also announced that there would be a larger staff meeting next week, and not to forget the party at three this afternoon. Glancing at his watch, Herb concluded with, "How about lunch? Let's meet in the lobby in half an hour."

I would always enjoy our unit lunches, frequently held at a nearby Chinese restaurant. That day was no exception, and I returned to the office ready for the O'Donnells.

Warren O'Donnell greeted me with a firm handshake as I entered the conference room where the couple sat. His wife, Beverly, smiled but did not rise or offer her hand. There was a formality about Mr. O'Donnell that was a bit uncomfortable, while his wife's quiet demeanor seemed to be a contrast to her husband's. She was a slender woman with medium brown hair that was cut in a somewhat plain, unbecoming style. She wore a subdued beige dress that did not flatter her coloring. In contrast, her husband's dark blue suit brought to mind the young executive on his way to the top.

"I'm sorry I wasn't in when you first called," explained Warren O'Donnell. "I am an auditor for several companies out of state. My work necessitates quite a few trips, and I happened to be on one when you called. Bev told me when I got home, and here we are." He smiled, obviously trying to put me at ease. He was a big man, and his size, let alone his formality, did not make him seem approachable. On to the task, I decided, and pulled out the pictures I had of Billy. Beverly looked on thoughtfully, smiling in her shy way.

"Wonderful!" boomed Warren O'Donnell. "I was hoping for a boy! When can we see him?" All business, I thought, and then remembered his profession. I guessed that he had to be task-oriented.

"Let me tell you a bit more about him," I said, and launched into my description of the baby. Beverly fingered the pictures quietly, and it was hard to read the thoughts behind her gray eyes. I hoped that it was appreciation and the beginnings of love. Her husband took out a date book and thumbed through it.

"Let me see," He scrutinized the book. "I am around next week and could take some time off if we could meet him then." We agreed that they could meet Billy on Tuesday with a possible placement on Thursday, if all went well.

"Well, that's settled then," concluded Warren, and I felt dismissed. He repeated his handshake, and this time Beverly also offered hers. They were gone in several minutes, and I felt as though I had been audited. I thoughtfully scooped up my papers and returned to my desk trying to figure out what I thought of the O'Donnells.

"Something wrong?" asked Herb, who happened to be talking to Deirdre at the next desk to mine.

"I don't know," I answered. "This couple just gave me a funny feeling."

"Can't like them all," Herb threw back. "It will be fine, I'm sure." I was glad that he was sure, because I wasn't.

The next day, I had two introductions scheduled. In the morning, the Devers were coming in to hear about Gabby, and in the afternoon, the Van Dykes were flying in to learn more about Skipper. I was excited about both meetings, and looking forward to them. As I returned to my desk to prepare for the Devers, a secretary motioned that I had a call. Denise Foreman greeted me with a less than cheery hello.

"I thought you might like to hear the latest. We met with Dolores' attorney and the decision has been made to return both Tina and Kevin to their mother," Denise told me.

"So soon?"

"Yup. Mom said that she had to get back home, so she is taking them both with her on Friday. It makes me nervous that she'll be several states away, but we are notifying the Department of Social Services in West Virginia. That's where she lives now. Once we give the kids back, it won't be an official notification, just a courtesy thing, I guess, and we'd feel better if someone down there knew what was up," Denise explained.

"What about Tina's foster parents?"

"They are pretty upset," she told me. "I don't think they'll ever take another foster child, or apply to be foster parents in the next state they live in."

"How about the kids?"

"Tina's pretty upset, too. She really wanted to move with her foster parents. Kevin thinks it is a big adventure. I think both of them remember what it was like with Mom before, but kids want to hope for fairy tale endings. We've got to hope for those ourselves in this case. Just thought you'd like to know."

I thanked Denise, saying a prayer that the Fontaine children would inspire their mom to live up to her promises for their care. Almost a year to the date, Denise would receive a call from the West Virginia child protection agency to let her know that the Fontaine children had again been taken into care. Gone was Tina's opportunity to be adopted by loving foster parents. Not only had we no idea of how to reach them, but the red tape of a three state placement would have been extremely difficult. Denise and I found small comfort in the fact that we had tried to make Tina's and Kevin's life a bit better. Now it was out of our hands.

Jeannine and Bob Dever were all smiles when I greeted them in the lobby, elevating my mood significantly.

"It was all we could do to get out of the house without the boys," Jeannine told me, referring to her two sons. "They are so excited!"

"Maybe they got the message from you!" laughed her husband, giving her a loving hug. To me he added, "We have been so excited since you called, and Jeannine has been a bundle of energy. She and the boys have rearranged the baby's room three times in the last two days. You'd think we'd never had kids!"

"Come on, Bob! This is different. With the boys we were too caught up in worrying about whether they would have two heads or all their fingers and toes. This time, it's different. We know that Gabrielle is okay." She turned to me hastily. "Not that we wouldn't have loved the kids no matter what, but . . . well, you know what I mean."

"Maybe you had better tell us more about this little girl," began Bob. "Then Jeannine can relax."

Once again, I pulled out the pictures and told them about Gabby. Like the other couples and the children I had told them about, there was no doubt that the Devers wanted to meet her.

"She is so beautiful," breathed Jeannine Dever, almost in awe.

"And she looks like our son, Mark, when he was a baby," added her husband. "When can we met her?"

I explained that the foster parents were very attached to her, and that I would need a few days at least to prepare them. I tried not to emphasize their attachment too much, lest I make the couple feel guilty that they were taking the child away from the people who had been parenting her. I should not have worried about the Devers understanding.

"I cannot imagine how difficult it must be for them!" said Jeannine Dever. "This is a precious baby, and it looks like they have taken good care of her. Please let them know that we will love her just as they have." I assured her that I would, and we scheduled a meeting for early the next week.

Meeting with couples like the Devers, who seemed so enthused and who appeared to have such a complimentary relationship, elevated my spirits. I learned over the years that one of the most difficult aspects of social work is the seemingly barometric mood changes that one experiences. Some clients naturally bring out the positive feelings in their social workers, while others send you home dragging through the evening. This may well be why the turnover among protective workers is so high. In protective services there are fewer positive outcomes, and the toll on the social worker's emotional balance is great. Even in adoption, where the successes feel more abundant, the work can affect the lives of the workers. For example, later in my time with the adoption unit, the number of baby showers for social workers made us wonder if there was an epidemic of pregnancy. Someone finally figured out that the majority of the couples who came to us with fertility problems had planted secret fears in the minds of the female workers about their own fertility. Therefore, it was not surprising that decisions to begin families started almost on a subconscious level in the workers.

My meeting with the Van Dykes that afternoon was equally energizing. Thomas Van Dyke looked the part of a professor in my mind. He was bearded, which made up for the sparseness of his brown hair. He wore glasses, and the tip of a pipe protruding from his breast pocket brought to mind a thoughtful academic, puffing on his pipe and deeply involved in a weighty book. But I hoped that I never had to take notes in a classroom with Tom Van Dyke at the lectern. He spoke quickly, almost as if he could not get his words out fast enough before others rushed out in their wake. Laura, on the other hand, was slower and more thoughtful. She reminded me of a first grade teacher who spoke slowly and kindly, being sure that you understood what she had just said before she moved on. It was an interesting combination, and I could see how, if they didn't drive each other nuts, they would complement each other. The latter was definitely the case. Their eye contact and obvious respect for each other told me that this was a couple who had made their differences work in their favor.

I thanked them for making the trip, especially since I realized that Tom Van Dyke had had to make arrangements for his classes at this, a crucial time of the semester.

"You couldn't have kept us away," Laura smiled warmly, and I knew that she meant it. I told them about Skipper, trying to keep my admiration for the boy from influencing my description. I had underestimated Laura Van Dyke.

"He's really won you over, hasn't he?" she laughed, to my surprise. I would later find that this woman's intuitive sense would be invaluable in my placement of Skipper and his adjustment to their home.

"Yes, he has," I had to admit. "He is a sweetheart." I hoped that I had not influenced them, but suspected that they had already made a decision to see the child.

"When can we meet him?" asked Tom, as he looked at Skipper's picture again. We had arranged that the Van Dykes would be in Boston for two days, and I had tentatively scheduled a meeting with Skipper the next morning. I suggested this and they agreed, giving each other a hug as if to give an obvious sign that they were together on this.

"We promised to call the girls tonight and tell them. They will be so pleased," said Tom, as he took his wife's hand.

"Yes," continued Laura, "They were dying to come, but we said no. We thought that it was up to us to do this step alone." Again, her wisdom impressed me. So many couples want to involve their entire family from the outset. Yet, involving other children or relatives does not allow the couple the freedom to decide whether this feels right for them.

Since they were unable to rent a car at this busy time of year, and Skipper's foster home was in the suburbs, I offered to pick the Van Dykes up at their hotel the next morning. I would then drop them off at a restaurant near the foster home, and go and get Skipper. I dreaded driving to the city hotel, but I thought this would be the easiest for them. The streets were crowded with holiday shoppers, and traffic tie-ups were the norm. Red nosed Santas decked many corners, ringing their bells for donations. Store windows, often with animated scenes, delighted the hoards of children and adults who came daily to experience the excitement of the holidays. The Christmas season was in full swing. I usually parked my car at a lot just out of the city and took the MBTA, Boston's subway system, in to work. Not only were the inner city parking lots very expensive, but having my car on the outskirts saved me from some of the commuter traffic.

I was surprised when Laura Van Dyke declined my invitation.

"It's too busy at this time of year," she said. "Tell us where to meet you, and we will take the MBTA there. The Green Line is still the best one out, isn't it?" My surprise at her knowledge of the subway system must have showed. She laughed and told me, "I graduated from Boston University. It's been a while, but I think I can still find my way around."

So it was that I picked up the Van Dykes at the last stop on the Green Line and we set off to meet Skipper. Having left them at a Howard Johnson's, the restaurant many of us used for introductions of couples and children in those days, I arrived at Skipper's foster home.

Agnes LeBlanc came out to the car and greeted me cheerfully once again with the comment, "He's ready for you! He's a smart little kid and he knows something is up!" I wondered if she felt any trepidation about the meeting between Skipper and the couple who might well take him out of her life. Perhaps reading my thoughts she said, "It's been a zoo around here. My daughter is auditioning for the high school play, and the other kids get so wound up when the Christmas season rolls around. And I haven't even started my Christmas shopping!" I responded sympathetically as we went into the house to find Skipper. He greeted me with uncharacteristic shyness, his thumb in his mouth and a tattered stuffed animal in his hand.

"Where we going?" he asked, as if he would base his willingness to go on my answer.

"How about instead of ice cream, we get a great big sundae? I know a place that has twenty-six flavors of ice cream," I coaxed.

His eyes brightened. "Really?" he asked wide-eyed and obviously I had won his company.

"Skipper said that Bunny likes ice cream, too," Agnes told me with a wink. "He'd like to take his bunny." I quickly realized that the tattered yellow rabbit that looked suspiciously like the much loved but very worn Velveteen Rabbit that I had read about as a child, was his security object. Apparently Skipper was feeling a bit anxious about what we were not telling him.

"Well, tell Bunny he is very welcome to come!" I said, and Skipper withdrew his thumb and scrambled into his coat never letting go of Bunny. Obviously, he was more than ready to go.

On the way to the restaurant, I explained that we might see some friends of mine there. I hoped it was okay if they joined us. Skipper said that it was, but he was too busy quizzing me on the kinds of ice cream they might have to really take much notice of my strange questions. We settled ourselves into a booth and I read off what Skipper might have. After he had confidently given his order to the waitress, we chatted for a bit. At that moment, by pre-arrangement, the Van Dykes dropped by. It was the practice of the adoption unit at that time to allow couples to view children in a neutral setting. If they liked what they saw, they would be introduced as friends of the worker and have an opportunity to interact with the child. All this was designed to give the couple and child every chance to become comfortable with each other with a minimum of pressure. Yet I wondered how many children saw through our ruse and were too polite or too scared to say so.

Laura Van Dyke sat next to Skipper, and her husband next to me. It was clear that she had a way with children as she asked Skipper about Bunny and talked easily about the rabbit's history. I got the attention of the waitress, and the Van Dykes ordered ice cream, too. When the sundaes came, Laura helped Skipper as Tom interjected comments as well. When I felt that everyone was comfortable, I said that I had a call to make. Would Skipper be okay with them for a minute? No one seemed to mind, so Tom let me out and I went off for a leisurely call to the office, a trip to the ladies room, and anything else I could think of to give them some time alone together.

When I returned, there were smiles all around, and the conversation was focused on Skipper's big sister (the foster mother's biological daughter), who was auditioning for a play.

Suddenly Skipper, in his usual unpredictably perceptive manner commented, "So, are you auditioning to be my new parents?" Everyone was so surprised that there was a moment of silence. Then we all laughed at our inability to fool this special child. Laura was the first to recover.

"And what would you say if we were?" she asked.

Skipper though for a brief minute.

"Cool!" he said with a big smile lighting up his ice cream-covered face. We concluded that the meeting was a success.

Questions for Thought _____

1. What type of support do you need in a work setting? Are you someone who enjoys camaraderie with coworkers or prefers to work alone?

2. What do you think motivates foster parents to take foster children? What motivations might be healthy and what might not?

3. What was your initial impression of the O'Donnells? On what is this based?

4. How would you have reacted, had you been the worker assigned to the Fontaine case? What did you think might be the outcome? What do you think went wrong?

5. What was your initial impression of the Devers? How did they differ from the O'Donnells?

6. What was your initial impression of the Van Dykes? How do all the couples compare? Can you see strengths and weaknesses in each?

9

Sit-ins, Holidays, and Sad Thoughts

As I entered the elevator at the office several days later, I thought about all that was ahead of me. The next day I had arranged for the Devers to meet Gabby. The reception I got when I asked the foster parents if this would be a good day to take her for the introduction was less than cordial. I wasn't quite sure what to do about it, as I was now convinced that they would not offer the best permanent plan for Gabby while the Devers would. I tried to tell the Polinskis as much as I could about Gabby's potential adoptive parents, but it was obvious that they were not won over. I empathized with their feelings, but this did not seem to make a difference.

I would also have to talk to Herb about how the Van Dykes' placement would progress. Despite the fact that they would have loved to have Skipper for Christmas, Laura had suggested that the foster mother might like to spend this last holiday with him.

"We'll have him forever," she explained with compassion. "This one holiday should be hers."

In addition to the concern for the foster mother, it would be difficult for anyone to get reservations to fly out to Illinois, where the Van Dykes lived, during the Christmas season. Herb had suggested that I be the worker to fly out with Skipper, as I had the relationship with him. I was excited but a bit anxious at the prospect. What if something went wrong? I was so new at this, I thought. But the Van Dykes were an exceptional couple, and together, I thought we could make this placement work. Another task before me was to make flight reservations for Skipper and I for later in January. Then I would have to make several visits to prepare him, and to help the foster mother, competent though she was, accept that she would be losing a child of whom she had grown quite fond. And the next week or so would also involve placing Billy with the O'Donnells. I wondered if the baby would bring out more emotion in his quiet adoptive mother-to-be.

So involved was I in my own thought that I almost missed my floor. But when the elevator doors open, I was sure that I had. I was met with a sea of mostly female bodies, all sitting in various poses on the floor of the hall outside my office, a hall that also led to several other state offices. The din of voices was almost deafening, and I could hardly miss the placards emerging from the crowd. "Mothers unite!" "Don't starve our babies!" The messages screamed out at me as much as the incomprehensible words. I was unsure of how I was to get to my office door, and contemplated going back down the elevator and seeking out the back entrance that I had not as yet used. But the door of another elevator opened, and Millie and Zach stepped out. They surveyed the scene before them, looked at each other in apparent decision, and began to step gingerly through the crowd. Zach suddenly saw me and waved his arm in an encouraging gesture. If he called to me, it was impossible to hear. I followed the two workers a bit less resolutely, sure I would step on someone's fingers or toes. The crowd let us pass, apparently more intent upon a reaction from another firmly closed door that also opened off the hall.

Once inside our office, we all breathed a sigh of relief.

"What was that?" I asked.

Millie laughed. "I guess we just broke a picket line! I heard that the welfare moms were going to picket the Welfare office, but I didn't think they'd do it. They are protesting for higher benefits. Don't blame them really. I couldn't live on what they get!"

The remainder of the day proved a bit less exciting as we tried to stay out of the drama that was occurring in the hallway. There was a back entrance, and we used that for the duration of the sit-in. In our office, business went on as usual. Although, at that time, the Division was one section of the Department of Public Welfare, there was little interaction between the two sections. For a variety of reasons, the section of the Department of Public Welfare that dealt with dependent children was separated from the Assistant Payments (financial payments) section, and in 1980 became a separate department called the Department of Social Services.

As life continued in the Adoption Unit, Herb praised the work I had done with my families and instructed me in how to make plane reservations through the travel agency we used. As I finished the call that would send Skipper and I off on our adventure, Herb approached me.

"Just got a call from the worker on the Hunter case," Each case came to us through a referral from an area office much like the one in which I had first had a job interview. The area worker often continued to be involved in the case until the adoption process was well under way. The mom in the Hunter case had been meeting with an area office worker, and it was that worker for whom the mom had signed the adoption surrender. "April Hunter, the mom, wants you to talk with her before you place her baby. I guess she wants to make sure she made the right decision. She also may want some assurance that the family you chose will be right for the baby."

It was a somewhat unusual request, but obviously the other social worker had felt that it was important. Herb gave me the address, and I promised to see her as soon as I could. I also had to see Jessica Barton before the court hearing and assess her for her readiness for adoption.

"She might be a good one to write up for the Santa Fund," Herb suggested.

"The what?" I asked.

"Every year at Christmas, we do little write ups on children to give to the radio station. Don't use real names and make sure the child could not be identified," he cautioned. "The write-ups are read on the air as a way to solicit donations for Christmas gifts for the kids. Oh, that reminds me. You should be making out a list of the children on your caseload and getting an idea from the foster mothers just what they would like for Christmas. The Department gives each child a gift. It's up to you to pick it out for your kids, buy it, wrap it, and deliver it. It's kind of fun. You'll get the hang of it." Herb told me.

This was my first introduction to Christmas as a social worker. In an attempt to bring a bit more joy to the lives of the children in our care, the Christmas present project became quite time consuming. Not only was it necessary to buy, wrap, and deliver gifts to the children on one's own caseload, but several donation boxes located in several malls and public areas had to be cleaned out regularly. We rotated performing that duty. I found it somewhat sad as I took my turn at this duty, how some people donated broken and unusable gifts to the children that they apparently assumed deserved nothing more. And yet, the only problem that many of these children had was their parent's inability to properly parent them. Somehow I felt these kids deserved more, not less, of the public's generosity. There were other gifts that attested to their donors' understanding of the plight of dependent children, and I blessed them for their thoughtfulness.

Another truth I was to learn about being a social worker at holiday time was that I rarely got my own shopping done until the very last minute. Crisis rides into the Christmas season along with Santa, and it would seem that many of my cases were affected. Children acted out. Biological parents wondered if they had made the right decision by giving up their children. Foster parents begged not to have you place their children before the holidays and adoptive parents pleaded just as convincingly to have their new sons or daughters to celebrate the holidays with them.

Amidst the confusion, I had my cases worked out. I would place Billy with the O'Donnells before Christmas, but wait until just after to place Gabby with the Devers and to make my trip to the Van Dykes with Skipper. But my plans had to be altered a bit when I learned that Mr. O'Donnell would be away until Christmas, and then the O'Donnells were expecting company throughout the holidays. Better to start afresh in January anyway, I reasoned. In the meantime, I arranged to see both April Hunter and Jessica Barton.

April lived in an upscale suburban neighborhood about an hour out of the city. My knock at the door of the attractive cape style home was answered by a lovely girl who extended her hand with a good deal of poise.

"Hi, I'm April," she greeted. She was slender, attesting to the fact that she had apparently lost any of the weight that she must have gained in pregnancy. She wore a lilac T-shirt and jeans, and moved with a certain grace. Her dark complexion was smooth and flawless, and her hair long and pulled back behind her ears. It was quite straight, and I suspected that she had used the hot iron that many Black girls used to straighten their hair at that time. She ushered me into a living room that seemed to double as a music room. A violin and bow sat on the couch, and a large piano took up one corner of the room. A large festive Christmas tree occupied most of the remainder of the space. Already, brightly decorated packages had been arranged under its heavy bows.

"I was just practicing," she explained, indicating the violin. "I have gotten kind of rusty. I didn't want to do anything right after Tara was born." There was a catch in her voice as she mentioned the baby that she had released for adoption. "Isn't her name pretty? I love the book *Gone With the Wind*. It's from that. The name of Scarlett's house, you know?"

I told her that I had loved the book also, had seen the movie several times, and that it was a beautiful name.

"It was hard, you know, giving her up," I could see the pain in April's eyes and I knew that it had been difficult for the young high school girl.

"Daddy wants me to go to college," she continued. And then she brightened. "I have a music scholarship. I don't think I could have gone with Tara." She seemed to be looking for my approval of her decision. Before I had a chance to respond, she went on.

"And then there was Stephen. That's Tara's father. I love him, you know. He would have stood by me. He wanted me to keep her, but our families," She looked at me plaintively. Then sensing that I did not understand, she said quickly, "Let me show you his picture. Then you will know what I mean."

She took from a nearby purse a photo that was much like the pictures taken for high school yearbooks. I suspected that it was the boy's senior picture. From the photo smiled a handsome boy with blonde curly hair and piercing blue eyes.

"He has a scholarship to Princeton," she said proudly. "He is a very good student. And he plays the trumpet. I play the flute as well as the violin, and we met in the band. He's a wonderful person." She looked at the photograph, and I could see the glistening of tears in her eyes.

I was startled. Tara's record listed her as Black and I had not suspected that her father was White. It suddenly became clear the difficulty that Tara had caused for these two young people. Despite some relaxing of societal prejudices, the 1960s were still difficult for mixed race couples. I could just imagine how these two talented, bright young people, in the height of their idealism, had found each other, only to come up against the pressures of parents and a society that had not quite learned to accept people for who they were, independent of their skin colors.

"My going to college means so much to Mama and Daddy. And Stephen's mother, she's a widow and he's her only child," she trailed off, trusting me to understand the implications. "So everyone thought it would be better for Tara." She began to cry softly, and I imagined how difficult the last few months had been for her.

"You did the right thing," I heard myself saying to ease her pain.

"Please find her a good family," she said through her tears. "She's such a wonderful baby. I was never sick at all when I was pregnant. She always tried to make it easy for me." Now her sobs were deeper, and I found my heart going out to her. I vowed to take special care to see that baby Tara had as loving an adoptive home as her young mother might have given her. Finally, April was able to dry her tears and talk about her music and her future. She seemed to have decided that I would do the best for Tara. I left promising to call her when Tara was adopted, and give her as much information about the adoptive family as I was allowed by agency policy. She seemed comforted, and as she stood in the doorway waving goodbye to me, I hoped that April Hunter could find some peace in her music and in her new life at college next fall.

When I presented a baby whose mother had relinquished him or her because mom was not married, most couples pictured a poor little high school girl like April, from a good family and with a bright future. In fact, April was the exception rather than the rule. The moms of most of the young babies that I placed for adoption often had their own stories of hardship far beyond becoming pregnant too early. Many were victims of sexual abuse, or from alcoholic families. Some went on to have other babies that I would place. April stood out for me, not because I had any less compassion for the other moms, but because it felt, in April's case, that there but for the grace of God go I. I had had loving parents who wanted the best for me. I had gone to college, not necessarily because I had wanted to, but more because I knew that it was important to them. This identification with Tara's mom had an impact on me as I set off for my next visit. I was scheduled to see Tara in her foster home, and now I almost wished that I had not made this appointment the same day that I had seen her mom.

I arrived at Tara's foster home with some trepidation. The foster mother, Mrs. Early, greeted me warmly. She was efficient, and bustled about getting me a cup of coffee and telling me that Tara would be awake soon. There were six small cribs placed around a large living room and I wondered at the arrangements.

"I only take the little ones who are about to be adopted," explained Mrs. Early with good humor. I was later to learn that she was known as the "Baby Lady" because she loved babies and took only the very young ones whose future seemed certain to be a speedy adoption. Her husband and her three married daughters, the latter coming in daily from their own homes, pitched in and helped her out with the feeding, diapering, and general care of her charges. It was a bright, cheerful atmosphere, and many times in my stay at the Adoption Unit I would hear both workers and adoptive parents sing the praises of this amazing woman. Mrs. Early took great pains to dress and groom the babies on the day that they went to their new families. Each baby was accompanied by a personal note from the foster mother, a new toy as a gift from her, and careful detail about their schedules, likes, dislikes, and personality. There was also a little scrapbook with pictures and notes about the baby's life since he or she had been with Mrs. Early. I never knew how she could get to know all the infants in her care, but she certainly did. New adoptive parents marveled at the way their baby was presented to them with such love and care. As I got to know this woman, I was thankful that Tara was in her care.

The soft cries from a nearby crib let us know that Tara was ready to join us. Two of the other babies decided to wake at the same time, and a young woman and an older man, Mrs. Early's daughter and husband, miraculously appeared and whisked away the other babies so that we could talk. Another baby cooed in a musical baby swing, and the two remaining babies were still asleep.

Tara was cute as babies go, though nothing like one might assume when described by the loving mother. Nor did she do justice to her two attractive parents. She was lighter complected than her mom, with a mop of tight black curls and deep brown eyes.

"She's a good baby," Mrs. Early was saying. "She'll make someone a lovely daughter. Do you have anyone in mind?"

I told her that since the mom had just signed the adoption surrender, the paperwork was still to be processed, but I assured her that I would be looking for a family as soon as I returned to the office.

"Her other social worker said that Mom had a hard time letting her go," shared Mrs. Early, and I wondered if she had any idea how tough it had been for April.

We continued to talk as Mrs. Early changed Tara and started to give her a bottle. About then, another baby whimpered and the foster mother asked if I would like to finish feeding Tara. As I held the small bundle and looked into her deep brown eyes, I whispered to her "Little baby, do you know how much you were loved?" She eyed me pensively and I hoped that somewhere in her baby mind, she had taken in my words.

I thought of April and Tara and Stephen as I celebrated my own Christmas. Amidst the warmth of my family, the scrumptious food, and the numerous gifts, I hoped that April and Stephen would find some peace and good will. I vowed again to look for someone special for baby Tara, and I tried to enjoy the blessings that were mine.

Questions for Thought

1. How would you have felt being faced with the welfare mothers' sit-in? How might you have reacted?

2. How would you have felt about April Hunter's request? Would you have complied? Why?

3. How would the commotion around the holidays affect you, considering there is little time for one's own personal celebration?

4. What was your impression of April Hunter? How might you have felt about working with her?

5. What was your impression of Mrs. Early? What might have been her motivation?

10

The Lull and Then the Storm

No one really wants to see a social worker during the week between Christmas and New Year's. Some of my Jewish colleagues argue that they work throughout their holidays, but the reality is that, other than a foster home visit or two to do routine first-time assessments, we stuck pretty close to the office or took a few days off for our own holiday. Since I had not earned that much vacation time yet, I busied myself catching up on dictation after a not-so-gentle nudge from Herb. On Tuesday, I received a call saying that Jessica Barton's foster mother did not feel she could keep her anymore.

"She has tantrums and was impossible over Christmas," the harried foster mother told me over the phone. "We really need to have her moved. She cannot disrupt the household like she does. I have other children to think of as well."

As I glanced at the record, I realized that this was the third foster home Jessica had been in since she had come into care a year ago. Each time, her foster parents had asked that she be moved because they could not handle her behavior. She was unreasonable in her demands, had difficulty in bonding with anyone, and had nightmares after which she could not be consoled. She was also described as sneaky, and had hurt family pets when the foster parents' backs were turned.

Today we might recognize Jessica's symptoms as indicative of attachment disorder, a difficulty that many severely abused children sometimes develop. Attachment disorder children never bond properly to their abusive caretakers, resulting in an inability to bond with anyone else later in life. They can also become manipulative and seemingly cruel as they try desperately to get their own needs met with the paradoxical expectation, based on their early experience, that no one can meet them. Now we know that such children need intensive therapy to help them to trust and to learn to attach to others. In these early years of my career, we had not yet discovered how many children would come to us for placement locked in their own little worlds. This may also account for some of the adoption failures, situations when adoptive parents and children are never able to adjust to each other, that marked each agency's statistical logs. I was to experience several similar cases myself. It is heartbreaking to watch a family that so desperately wants the love of their adopted child be locked out by the residual effects of the nightmare that was that child's first years on Earth.

All I knew at that moment was that Jessica needed another foster home, and quickly. Zach was the first worker I saw.

"Help!" I appealed to him, explaining the situation.

"How about Mrs. R?" he suggested, using his fond name for Mrs. Riley. "She's great with tough kids, and no one has placed another child with her since Julie left."

"Super!" I said in relief, and after securing agreement from the foster mother, Zach and I arranged to move Jessica that afternoon. Before we left, Herb suggested that we attempt to fill in the blank spaces in the record, so that we knew what the little girl had experienced.

It was a bizarre feeling sitting around my supervisor's office with two men, Zach and Herb, discussing what type of sexual deviations might have been perpetrated on this child. As I tried to remain clinical and not give in to the embarrassment caused by my youth, my incredible naiveté, and the mores of the day when sex was not discussed as easily as it is today, I vowed to make sure that Gertie was not the typist on any of my other cases.

"How can she do this?" I asked incredulously.

"If she is grossed out by a word, she just leaves it out. We have spoken to her and spoken to her, but to no avail," explained Herb.

Discussing what had happened to Jessica in vivid detail made me feel somehow tainted. I was glad that I did not have to go into detail with Mrs. Riley, but just needed to have some idea myself what we were up against in helping this child heal. I would have nightmares too if I had experienced what she had. I was glad that she would be moving to the home of a caring foster mother.

Jessica's old foster mother greeted us guiltily.

"I'm really sorry to ask you to take her. I've never asked to have a child removed before, but this one really has problems." She led us into a playroom where Jessica sat on the floor playing with some dolls. She didn't look up when we entered but continued, seemingly unconcerned, to go about her play.

"I have her all packed," the foster mother told us.

She dressed Jessica in a snowsuit, and the child was compliant enough.

"She can be so engaging," the flustered caretaker said, seemingly in defense. She smiled at Jessica. "I'm sorry, honey," she told her. "But this is for the best."

I noticed that there were tears in her eyes when we left, and I suspected that it was difficult for this mother to feel that she had failed a child. Yet, not every child fits into every home. I hoped that it would be better for Jessica with Mrs. Riley.

The ride to Mrs. Riley's was quiet, with Jessica playing in her car seat in the back. Mrs. Riley greeted us with her usual enthusiasm, and asked Jessica if she could help her get out of her things. The child nodded complacently.

"Let me show you your room," she invited, when the snow suit had been hung in the closet. After looking at the room, Jessica sat on the floor of her room and continued to play with the doll that she had brought with her. There seemed to be no devotion to the toy in her play, but rather a methodical dressing and undressing of the small plastic body.

Mrs. Riley, Zach, and I went back into the parlor and discussed Jessica in low tones. I told her honestly about the cruelty to animals, the changes between engaging, complacent, and anti-social behavior, and the nightmares.

"Sounds like this little one will need a lot of tender loving care," she concluded, not at all daunted by the task. In later months, this dedicated foster mother would do wonders for Jessica, but it was difficult to repair the damage that had been done to her psyche. The petition to terminate parental rights would be allowed, and at five, she would finally be placed for adoption, only to have it fail two years later after the adoptive family no longer felt that they could handle her behavior. After a series of foster homes, Jessica would eventually be placed in residential treatment, and it was there that I lost track of her. Hopefully the Jessicas of today might fare better. We have learned more about attachment disorder, and now have ways in which to reach such children. But how many Jessicas were there, the unhappy adults who grew up in foster care because we did not know how to make up for the abuse they had suffered?

New Year's Eve came and went. My dating life had been on hold since I started working. I had not been without dates in college, but since I returned home, there had been no one special. I realized, as I spent a quiet New Year's Eve with my parents, that my job had taken up a good deal of my emotional energy. How could one not get involved with these children? It is not surprising that there are numerous office romances among social workers. The job is such that spare time is at a minimum. In later years, I would find myself involved with several fellow social workers. This can be both healthy and unhealthy. Although you may understand the demands placed on your partner, it is sometimes nice to talk with an intimate who is not as involved in social work as you are. I vowed to broaden my horizons in the future. When I did eventually marry, it was to someone who had little to do with social work.

January brought with it a snap of very cold weather. I was glad that my little Volkswagen had an especially overzealous heater as I drove out to Gabby's foster home. This was the day that I would bring the adorable little girl out to meet the Devers for the first time. We had arranged to meet at a restaurant that was not far from the foster home. I hoped that the management had an abundance of hot coffee.

I had talked with the Polinskis several times in an attempt to prepare them for this day. I was obviously not welcome anymore as they struggled to face the reality of Gabby's leaving. But I thought I had done a good job of convincing them that the Devers were one in a million, and this was the right move for Gabby. I was again greeted by a flourish of high-pitched barks and no other response. When the dogs would not cease their cacophony, the door was finally opened by Herman, who without a greeting turned to resume whatever was his task. As he left the door open, I assumed that I could go in and did so. I was surprised to see Gabby still in her pajamas and toddling around with an exceptionally dirty face that bespoke of the breakfast offerings. I glanced at my watch, sure that I had told Mrs. Polinski the correct time. She was doing dishes and had her back to me. She gave me a curt hello and turned back to the dishes, running water noisily. Gabby also did not greet me with the enthusiasm she had on the last few visits. I looked to Herman, wondering where I might get support and observed that he was busily engaged in cleaning a rather menacing looking shotgun. Wonderful, I thought. A message?

Finally deciding that the only alternative was to take the matter into my own hands, I said to Mrs. Polinski, "Would you like me to help you get her dressed?"

"Suit yourself," she mumbled, with no apparent attempt to help me.

"Gabby, can you show me your clothes?" I asked. She wordlessly led me to what was apparently her bedroom, judging from the pink animals parading across the walls. She perched herself on the bed, watching me open her dresser drawers in search of an outfit. It seemed she was not willing to be any more helpful than her foster mother. I chose an appropriate outfit and spied a bathroom where I found a wash cloth and towel, with which I managed to return the grubby little girl back to the appearance of her angelic self. This all felt very presumptuous in someone else's home, but the Polinskis had apparently drawn the battle lines, and I was willing to comply. A thoroughly different child gazed back at me when I had her all washed and dressed.

"Let's go out and do something special," I encouraged, taking her hand. She gave it to me hesitantly, and followed me out into the parlor again. The scene had not changed. The Polinskis were each at their original posts.

"Does she have a snow suit?" I asked, with new resolve that they would cooperate.

"Over there," gestured the foster mother. I dressed the child, carefully insuring that all that was exposed was her cute little face.

"I'll have her back soon," I told them as I hoisted Gabby into my arms and left the house. As soon as the door closed behind us, she began to cry. Her cries intensified on my walk to the car until she was screaming and thrashing in my arms. It was all I could do to hold her. Her wails of what seemed like pure terror must have registered on the other side of the still closed door. Her scream became louder. I almost dropped her as I tried to get hold of my door handle and retain my hold on the flailing bundle. I felt like a kidnapper. It was clear that whatever had been said to Gabby frightened her terribly. I tried talking to her calmly, but my words could not be heard above her screams. I looked down at her only to discover that there was foam now forming around her mouth. I could take it no longer.

"Okay Gabby," I said trying to sound gentle. "You don't have to go with me. We'll go back inside." The wails turned to whimpers and the struggling stopped as I opened the door of the house almost knocking over Mrs. Polinski despite her size, as I threw open the door. Her look was one of unmasked "I told you so!"

"I will call you," I shot back, unsure of how to handle the situation. I got back in my car, drove down the long driveway, turned onto the main road and pulled over at the nearest rest area. And then I let the tears flow. I sat there sobbing until a trucker pulled up beside me and looked into my car.

"You okay?" he mouthed soundlessly. I nodded, tried to dry my tears and put the car into gear. I would find a phone and call Herb. I had no idea what to do next.

I blessed Herb for being there and not in a meeting when he answered the phone. "What's up?" he asked.

I tearfully explained what had happened and he listened quietly.

"My first reaction would have been, get her in the car and calm her down there," he said. "But this kiddo was abused, and may remember on some level being forced into doing what she did not want. You did right. Let the situation calm down and we'll talk about it when you come into the office tomorrow."

I was thankful for his calm and understanding of how the experience had affected me. As I was about to hang up, he said,

"And Cindy?"

"Yes."

"Relax. You did fine." Which brought another flood of tears, but this time in relief.

I got some lunch and tried to calm down after my morning. Next, I was scheduled to pick up Billy and take him to meet the O'Donnells. I actually looked forward to the understated emotional tone that I had come to expect from Mrs. O'Donnell. I was almost wishing that I was going to Mrs. Riley or Agnes LeBlanc's foster homes. I could imagine telling either of them that it had been a tough morning, without going into detail and being rewarded with a fresh cup of coffee or cookies. But Billy's foster mother was friendly and efficient, and in no time, he was ready to go. The meeting with the O'Donnells was as I had expected. Mr. O'Donnell's deep voice frightened Billy at first, but he seemed to warm to his potential adoptive father. Mrs. O'Donnell was her usual quiet self, but did the obligatory things that one does with a baby. At the close of the meeting, Mr. O'Donnell asked when Billy could be delivered, which made him sound like a package. We agreed upon the next Monday, and we all set off in our separate cars. Billy cooed at me from his car seat on the return to the foster home, and I wondered what it would be like to have a baby of my own. The day ended much better than it had begun, but I could not help thinking about Gabby and wondering what we would do.

Back in the office the next day, Herb and I discussed the possibilities.

"Do you think that the Devers could win over the foster family?" Herb asked me unexpectedly. I thought of Jeannine Dever's smile, and the couple's obvious devotion to each other. Both were warm and outgoing. They could not help but win over even the most reluctant and turn them into their fans.

"Sure, but what are you thinking?" I asked.

He smiled. "When all else fails, we punt. I suggest that we take the Devers to the foster home."

At that time, Herb's suggestion was a radical one. It was very rare that the foster and adoptive families would ever meet, and even more unusual to take a couple to a foster home. There were too many pitfalls, not the least of which is that the couple may feel guilty taking a child away from a home where he or she seemed so happy.

"If you feel sufficiently comfortable with this couple, you might explain to them that the foster parents are having a rough time. But they are older, and keeping Gabby is not an option. What do we have to lose at this point?"

I knew that he was right and quickly went to call the Devers. Fortunately, Jeannine was at home, and she had no problem with our plan. Mrs. Polinski was less than enthusiastic, but did agree to let the couple come for a visit. I guessed that she was secretly glad to get a look at these people who were threatening to take her Gabby. I suspected that she would also be critical, looking for any flaws she could find in the potential adoptive parents' characters.

The cold had eased up a bit the day that I met the Devers and joined them in their car (it was not common to use a couple's car, but my Volkswagen was a bit small for more than two people) for the trip to the Polinskis'.

"This must be so difficult for these folks," said Jeannine as we rode up the driveway. "I'm anxious to meet them and see where Gabby has lived so happily."

To my surprise, the door was opened at the slightest bark from Tinker and Petey, the canine sentinels. A smiling Mrs. Polinski greeted us, donned not in her usual housedress and somewhat bagging knee length nylons, but in a more attractive dress with no evidence of sagging hose.

"Come in," she offered with a brief look at me that I could not interpret. I, on the other hand, was feeling a bit annoyed. What was this? Kill them with kindness and show how incompetent the social worker is?

"What a lovely fire," purred Jeannine as she surveyed the blaze that warmed the room. The knickknacks had been neatened and the place was spotless. Herman, sitting in a chair before the fire with Gabby in his lap, responded to Bob Dever's hearty hello by putting down the little girl and rising to give his own hand. Before long, the two men were deep in conversation, and Herman was dragging Bob off to see his gun collection. I hoped that that was not a message similar to the one I felt he had given me with the shotgun. But from their manner with each other, I decided that it was more by way of male bonding.

Jeannine was already taking to Gabby, who smiled coyly and agreed readily to sit on her lap. Mrs. Polinski looked on, seeming not at all threatened by the interchange. I felt like a fifth wheel, but decided that I would just observe and hope for the best.

Mrs. Polinski had made coffee and offered us cookies while Jeannine produced a decorated cookie in the shape of a rabbit for Gabby.

"My sons made this for you," she told the child. "They would love to meet you."

Mrs. Polinski launched into a discussion of her son, giving no indication that he was no longer living. I hoped Jeannine did not stumble over this one. But she talked easily about her children, comparing notes and developing an easy rapport.

I wondered what we would do next when I heard Jeannine say, "We have so wanted a little girl. The boys have been such a joy but there is something about a girl that warms a mother's heart."

Careful Jeannine, I thought, but she apparently had everything under control. Gabby had toddled after the men who were now talking about dogs, and Jeannine leaned forward in almost a confessional style.

"We would love to have Gabby," she said quietly, and I held my breath. "But I know how hard this must be for you." And then she turned to me, saying, "If the

Polinskis would like, we could adopt them, too, like Gabby's grandparents. You could visit if you like, and we could write and perhaps call."

I wondered if Jeannine realized how she was throwing mud on Department etiquette. I couldn't imagine that the arrangement would ever get approved by the Department or be agreeable to the Polinskis. But to my surprise, Mrs. Polinski brightened. Jeannine turned to me and I was on the spot.

"Do you think that would be possible?" she asked with an engaging smile.

Today, such a suggestion would have been a possible alternative, but at the time, it was against what we usually did.

"I'll check it out," I answered feebly. And so, in that moment we changed Department policy. The Polinskis cooperated with the remainder of the placement process. After getting approval for the plan from Herb and his superiors, the Devers visited again, with me as chaperone, and got to take Gabby out with them. After another such visit, she stayed for a weekend, returned to the Polinskis', and the next weekend took up residence with her new adoptive family. They brought Gabby back to visit several times, and periodically the couples dropped cards and letters to each other. A year after Gabby became part of her new family, Herman Polinski suffered one more heart attack and died. Jeannine was immensely helpful in comforting the distraught foster mother, and they continued to have contact until Mrs. Polinski's own death eighteen months later. For Gabby, the transition had been made successfully, and she was quite content in her adoptive home. We all learned a lesson from this placement. Sometimes it was the clients who knew the best solutions.

Questions for Thought

1. How much have you learned about attachment disorder in your studies? Considering that a high percentage of children in foster care today have some degree of attachment problems, it is wise to learn about this topic. What symptoms of attachment disorder did Jessica Barton exhibit?

2. How might you have felt about Jessica's foster mother wanting her removal? What might you have said to her?

3. What might you have said to the Polinskis to prepare them for Gabby's leaving? What feelings might they have had?

4. How would you have handled the situation when you went to pick up Gabby?

5. What do you think of the eventual plan for Gabby's placement? What were the positive and negative points for the plan? What could have gone wrong?

6. What helped the Polinskis adjust to Gabby's placement?

11

A Flurry of Placements

January decided to cooperate and not burden us with too much snow. I was encouraged by the success of Gabby's placement and anxious to see Billy, Skipper, and Tara Hunter in new homes. On a cold morning in early January, I picked up a bundled up Billy and delivered him to the O'Donnells. Their home was a modest ranch in the western part of the state, a good two hours from Billy's foster home. He slept most of the way and when he was awake, I babbled on in my routine infant preparation speech that I hope he, like Jeremy, was taking in. The O'Donnells greeted me and showed me the room they had prepared for Billy. It was lovely, and made it obvious that Beverly O'Donnell had some artistic talent. Her husband seemed more comfortable with the baby than she did, but I chalked it up to her being an only child. He, on the other hand, was the oldest of six children. We unpacked the belongings that I had brought with Billy, and I left, anxious to get to my next appointment, new case, before the dark sky made good of its threat of snow.

The next morning found me in the office, searching in vain for a home for Tara Hunter. I looked through the card sort and discovered that we had a minimum of Black couples that had been approved for a baby. Of those we had, about half a dozen, all specified that they wanted a child who had been born to Black parents. Puzzled, I took my questions to Herb.

"It's not easy to place a mixed race child," Herb told me. "Most of the Black couples we have specify that the child should not be mixed. But many Black families keep children that are born to unwed mothers. It is a real dilemma. You might be better off looking for a white couple that will take a mixed race child."

It was puzzling to me why families would have strong feelings about race. A child was a child, and when one needed a home, that seemed to be the paramount consideration. I glanced through the cards of white couples that had specified that they would take a child of mixed race, wondering how April would feel. And then the ideal profile jumped out at me: Alexis and Willard Tyler. Wife: blonde hair, blue eyes, Swedish and English descent, Caucasian; husband: black hair, brown eyes, Black; preference for a child: girl preferred but boy accepted; mixed race preferred. Bingo!

The exact reverse of Tara's parents, the Tylers seemed to be ideal. After checking in with Herb, protocol that preceded any placement, I called the Tylers. No answer. Another look at the record told me that Willard worked for the Public Works Department and Alexis was an aide in a daycare center, mornings only. I made a mental note to call them in the afternoon.

Herb came by my desk with three other new cases and also suggested that I pick up my airline tickets for my trip to the Van Dykes the next week.

"You really think I can handle it?" I asked tentatively.

"You'll be fine," he reassured. "Look how you handled the Devers."

I laughed inwardly. It was more like the Devers handled me, I thought. But it all worked out.

I had prepared Skipper for his trip, and he was quite excited. The Van Dykes had sent him several notes and a Christmas card, including pictures of their daughters and the house in which they lived. Agnes LeBlanc, his foster mother, had done a wonderful job of preparing him as well. I think that she was so grateful when I told her that it was Laura Van Dyke's suggestion that Christmas with Skipper be hers, that she was making a special effort to make the placement go smoothly.

I picked up the tickets on my lunch hour, and prayed that the snow would hold off during my trip. Back at the office, I tried once again to get in touch with the Tylers. Success! A soft feminine voice answered after several rings. When I identified myself and said that we thought we had found a child for them, I was rewarded by her immediate enthusiasm.

"How perfect!" she said when I explained Tara's parentage. My thoughts exactly. We set up an appointment for several days later, and I thought of how relieved April would be. I considered calling her, but decided to wait until the placement was arranged.

When I met with the Tylers, I knew that April would have liked them. Will Tyler's broad smile reminded me of April, and Alexis' gentleness also brought her to mind. They were thrilled with the pictures and the description of baby Tara. They had no children, although there was no apparent reason why they had been unable to conceive. After trying for five years, they were thrilled that Tara was about to come into their lives.

"What a beautiful name," said Alexis, and I knew that I had chosen well. So it was that Tara Hunter became Tara Alexis Tyler. A year later, she would be joined by a baby brother, the first biological child of Alexis and Will. Despite the common belief that the best way to conceive is to adopt, this happens to only about eleven percent of all couples who adopt. I was sure that Tara would be loved as much as her new brother, and that April and Stephen would have been pleased with her new parents.

Chicago's O'Hare Airport was, as always, a sea of unfamiliar faces, but Skipper was enthralled. He had never been on a plane before, and clutching tightly to Bunny, his much loved stuffed toy, he had a question about every bit of the flight to his new adoptive home. We even got a tour of the cockpit when the plane landed for a layover in New York, and an attentive stewardess heard his numerous questions about how the miraculous machine could fly so high. It was a relief to have his questions answered by someone much more knowledgeable than I was. The sum total of my transportation machine knowledge was my ability to turn the key in the ignition of my Volkswagen and assume that it would start.

I was probably just as excited as Skipper. My air travel had been confined to the one or two trips I had taken to my college in Ohio. The rest of the time, I had taken the 24-hour train ride along with most of the other students I knew. I was pleased to be the envy of the office as the courier for an interstate adoption. I will admit to a bit of anxiety as Skipper darted in and out of hurrying strangers on our way to the gate. Whatever would I do if I lost him! I was relieved when I saw the smiling faces of Laura and Tom Van Dyke awaiting our arrival. Skipper saw them too, and waved, scampering through the gate and into Laura's arms. Great, I thought. No shyness on his part!

A ride punctuated by "how was your trip?" and "the girls are so excited," ended us in front of an attractive brick house on the outskirts of the city. Two attractive girls who I assumed were Megan and Sarah came out to greet us. Megan at fourteen was a graceful carbon copy of her mother, while twelve-year-old Sarah favored her father in both her looks and her ability to chatter. Tom gave us a running commentary on the house, the neighborhood and the area, while Skipper watched the girls as they, too, sized him up. Finally, Sarah was there beside us, admiring Bunny and chatting easily to Skipper, who seemed to relax. Megan followed suit, and before long they had volunteered to show Skipper where he was to sleep and disappeared with him in tow.

"Your motel is right down the street," Laura told me. We had decided that I would stay nearby, but would not leave until Skipper had gone to bed. I had visited him at his foster home numerous times as I was preparing him for placement, and he now saw me as a special friend. I was glad, as this would make his ability to become comfortable in this new setting easier with me as a transitional object of sorts. I half expected Skipper to want to come with me when Tom took me over to the motel to check in, but he was obviously engaged by the girls, and made no attempt to come with us. I had explained to him that I was staying nearby, which seemed enough for him.

Dinner was a pleasant, family-centered event, punctuated pleasantly by the fact that Laura was an excellent cook. The children played while I helped Laura clean up. As we returned to the family room, I noticed Megan and Sarah had engineered a slide show featuring family pictures of them when they were Skipper's age and younger. To my amazement, Skipper was enthralled both by the pictures and by the shadow creatures Sarah showed him could be made on the screen when the light shone on it. Before long, Skipper was yawning, and it seemed an appropriate time to initiate the bedtime ritual. Bunny was found wedged in the sofa cushion, and Laura and I joined together to get Skipper ready for bed. When both boy and rabbit were well tucked in, Laura suggested that she read him a story and I took this as my opportunity to leave to let Skipper and his new mother continue their bonding.

"He's a great kid," Tom greeted me downstairs. "The foster mother has done a super job with him. Was it terribly difficult for her to let him go?"

I said that it was difficult for her, trying not to instill guilt in the concerned adoptive father, but assured him that Agnes was a pro, and she was more interested in

Skipper's happiness than anything else. He asked if they could drop her a line, and remembering the Devers, I said it would be fine.

Laura was back in a surprisingly short time, and she looked a bit flustered.

"He wants you," she told me with a bit of concern. "And he is beating his bunny. I don't know what's wrong."

I found Skipper indeed beating Bunny and crying softly as he did.

"Skipper, what's wrong? Why are you hurting Bunny?"

The child turned his huge, tear-filled eyes up to me for a moment and said, "Bunny's been bad. He's a bad bunny and I am going to send him away!"

Suddenly, in my imagination, my child psychology textbooks were open before me and I was reading about this very scene. When children are removed from a home, they often feel that they have been sent away because they did something wrong. And here was Skipper, asking the forbidden question in metaphor as he acted out his fears on the beloved Bunny.

Filled with emotion for this precious little boy who had stolen my heart, I patiently explained that we didn't send away bad bunnies. We loved them and tried to understand. I finished by telling him that Mommy Agnes had not sent him away. She loved him very much. But she loved him so much that she wanted him to have a forever home here with the Van Dykes. I suggested that we call Agnes the next day, and he seemed calmed. Bunny was allowed to be cuddled again to soothe his wounds, and Skipper quietly fell asleep on my shoulder.

The next day, after a call to Agnes, who assured him that he was loved and told him how exciting it was that he had a new Mommy and Daddy who would love him forever, Skipper invited Laura to put him to bed after he had said good night to me. Two days later I was back on a plane to Massachusetts, bidding Skipper and his new family goodbye, thankful that I had found such a special family for such a special child.

That next Christmas, a card with a family picture arrived with fair-haired Megan and Laura, and dark-haired Tom, Sarah, and Skipper smiling out at me. I had received several other cards since the placement, and all indicated that Skipper was doing well. Several more Christmases brought much-awaited pictures of Skipper and his sisters as they grew, until Megan went way to college and the picture cards stopped. Almost twenty years later, when I was busy with my own children, a letter would find me, forwarded through several offices and finally delivered by a friend who knew me, from a Kenneth Van Dyke. At first the name meant nothing, and then it all came back to me. Kenneth "Skipper" Van Dyke had sent a clipping of his graduation from college and a note that read

"I don't know if I ever thanked you for giving me the family that you did, but thanks! We have talked about you over the years, and wondered how many children like me you had placed. I hope this gets to you. I took a chance that you might still be a social worker. My sisters and parents say hi, too. Best of luck to you." And it was signed, Kenny, a.k.a. Skipper.

In a tearful moment as I read it, I thought of the little boy who had won my heart. I was glad that his had been one of the success stories.

Questions for Thought _____

1. Would you have had any particular impressions of Billy's placement in the O'Donnell's home?

2. What was your impression of the Tylers?

3. How would you have felt making the long distance placement of Skipper?

4. Would you have handled Skipper's initial adjustment any differently?

5. How can a child be helped to handle separation? How would you explain it to a child? What factors must be considered?

12

An Act of God?

It was a busy winter. My caseload grew as more and more children became available for adoption. Tired of the winter commute of over almost two hours from my parents home and anxious to be on my own, I found a small apartment in the Boston area where I stayed when in the office or when my appointments were closer to that area. I also enjoyed being at the apartment on weekends, when the excitement of Boston and new friends was much more exhilarating for someone in their early twenties than was the quiet of my parents' small town. It was not long before I began to consider my apartment home and my parents' house a place to visit.

I continued my supervisory visits with the Devers, the Tylers, and the Ragusas. All seemed to be doing quite well with their adjustments. The psychologist had been out to test little Jerry Ragusa and called me with the results. Having children tested psychologically after placement was a service that we provided, especially if we had any questions that the child might have learning disabilities later in childhood. Jerry's slow development and early seizure made him a candidate for such a service.

"You'll never believe this," said our psychologist, Martha Foster, when she had seen Jerry. "That kid is testing well above average. And this was the kid we thought might have been slightly mentally retarded when he was a very young infant!"

When I told Herb, he chuckled.

"That's what a lot of love can do for you!" he told me. "I've seen it happen before."

Gabby Dever was enjoying her big brothers, who considered her their personal project. She and her next older brother had their moments, Jeannine told me, but they usually were able to work it out. The Tylers were still marveling at Tara's development and, since I had told them of her parents' musical talents, were convinced that she would be a musician.

Herb had given me several more cases, including Gavin, a baby addicted to heroin at birth. My supervisor told me to do assessment visits on all of the new cases, but talk with him before I went to see the drug addicted child. Children addicted to drugs at birth presented special problems in their prognosis for the future. The drugs ingested by their mothers in pregnancy had permanently imprinted their small systems. Not only did they go through withdrawal at birth, but they were likely to be hypertensive, startle easily, have eating difficulties, and a myriad of other problems. Some babies developed seizures and had learning difficulties later in life. I knew that this case would take a bit of time to secure just the right placement.

Feeling that there was not enough time to get to all that I must get done, I complained that I needed a few more hours in the week. Herb then reminded me that my dictation was again overdue, and would I please catch up. I groaned.

"Maybe I will just have to work on Saturday," I threatened. Herb gave me a dirty look and returned to his office. As I contemplated how I would ever get ahead of the work, I thought, why not? Maybe working Saturday was the way to get in another day. I poked my head into Herb's office. He was busily reading a file.

"Herb? What if I did work next Saturday?"

He looked up, frowning.

"I'm against it," he said, and returned to his file.

"Does that mean 'no'?" I asked, realizing that I was still dependent on my supervisor's permission.

"I can't prevent you," he said, not even looking up. "But I'm against it." The subject seemed to be closed in his mind. Alright, I thought. I don't have to depend on my supervisor for permission. I'll do it! I mentally reviewed who I could visit on Saturday.

The two foster mothers of my new cases seemed surprised at my choice of day, but agreed that I could come. Both homes were in the far western part of the state and I decided that my extra day was a good time to get out there. The O'Donnells' was out that way too, I realized, and I could make a supervision visit to them.

I had visited the O'Donnells' a week after their placement, and felt that they were doing fine. The snow and ice of winter had prevented me from getting out to their distant home as much as I liked, but in late March, the weather was a bit better. Since I would be out in their direction anyway, I scheduled another visit. Predictably, Bev O'Donnell told me that Warren was away, but I assured her that seeing just her and the baby would be fine. They had changed Billy's name to David and I tried to get used to the name change. Many couples of infants change the name to one that they have chosen. Older children tended to retain their names rather than giving them one more issue to impede adjustment.

It was the time of year that I dreaded when the world appeared gray. Old snow had turned to sandy, muddy slush that coated cars and obscured license plates. Windshield wipers and cleaning fluid were the most valuable additions to the car, as passing vehicles splattered you with goop that obscured your vision until you could hastily engage the windshield wipers for another swipe. Easter and the first day of spring were not far away, and I hoped that the spring flowers would be close behind. This had been the first winter that I was a full time driver, and it had convinced me that winter, except when one could be on the ski slopes, was not my favorite time of year.

I visited the two new foster homes and decided that these relatively young and healthy infants would be easy to place. In mid-afternoon I arrived at the O'Donnells'.

Beverly O'Donnell greeted me in a somewhat baggy housedress. I almost wondered, from her appearance, if she remembered that this was the day of our visit. My, how she had changed, I thought, as she opened the door wider to let me in. Once a slender woman, she had put on an amazing amount of weight. Her affect, never particularly enthusiastic, seemed even more subdued. Billy/David was sitting in a high chair and seemed not to take notice of my presence. His formerly blonde curls were plastered to his head with whatever he had been eating. He pushed several cheerios around the tray with apparent disinterest. The odor in the room suggested that he was also over-due for a change.

Mrs. O'Donnell offered me coffee, hardly acknowledging her son. We sat over our coffee and I tried to put my finger on the uneasy feeling that filled me. My question of "How are things going?" was met with her uttering the appropriate response that all was going well despite the fact that her affect did not seem to say that all was well. Billy/David continued with his ineffectual and seemingly lethargic pursuit of Chee-rios®, paying little attention to us. Had he grown thinner, or was it my imagination?

As we talked, I was more and more aware of the odor that pervaded the room. Finally, I wrinkled my nose and said that I wondered if the baby needed a change.

"He probably does," said Bev O'Donnell, with no apparent offense at my hav-ing pointed it out to her. With what seemed to me like reluctance, she picked up her son and took him into another room, where I assumed she was changing him. In a moment, she returned and plunked the child in a waiting playpen with a few toys, then returned to talk to me. Why did it seem that she was more interested in my visit than in displaying her motherhood skills? Billy/David ignored the toys, but contented himself with gazing complacently at the pattern on the pad of the playpen.

"Is David a pretty good eater?" I asked feebly, a combination of not knowing what else to say and needing to know why the baby had grown so thin.

"He's not that great an eater," answered Bev, and I remembered Billy's foster mother talking about how well the baby ate. Children did go through stages, I knew. Perhaps this explained the change.

When it seemed that there was nothing else that I could ask or add, I left, feel-ing that there was something else to be said. I had no idea what it was. Bev O'Donnell had always been somewhat quiet. Perhaps it was my imagination that she seemed even more subdued and almost depressed. I vowed to make my next visit a bit sooner than normal, just to keep an eye on the situation.

It was late afternoon as I drove the long route back home, and I thought of the evening ahead. I had considered stopping off for a visit to my parents, but a friend's invitation to a party sounded more inviting. I realized that a slight drizzle had begun, and hoped that I would reach Boston before the temperature dropped any more. March could still be unpredictable. The day was overcast, and the shadows of dusk were just beginning. The Saturday night traffic of people about to enjoy a night out had not yet begun, and there were few cars on the road. I thought about the O'Donnells. What was it that gave me the uneasy feeling? I looked forward to sharing the case with my colleagues and getting their take on it. A massive semi truck barreled past me, spray-ing my car with muck. Grumbling, I turned on my wipers full force. Suddenly, my car bucked and swerved as a huge object crashed into me, temporarily obscured my vision, rolled over my car, and with another bang, rolled off to one side. Shocked by the jolt and the fact that my small car was slowing to a stop, I instinctively looked to the offender trying to figure out what had hit me. The semi was speeding into the distance, its license, which I had the presence of mind to search for, was obscured by a thick layer of grime. Off to my side, a gigantic spare tire rolled down the hill and bounced into a guardrail, sending it back into the road. Fortunately, there were no other cars to be ambushed by its uncontrolled path. The scraping and lopsided weaving of my Volkswagen Bug let me know that there was significant damage, and with effort, I pulled to the side of the road. Almost as soon as I reached the side of the road, the car stalled. Shaken, I tried to reconstruct what had happened, and realized that the spare tire of the semi had apparently come loose and had crashed into the front of my small car. It then rolled over me and must have also done some damage to the engine, contained in the rear of the Volkswagen.

After a moment to calm myself and assess that I was unhurt, I pulled my coat more tightly around me and got out to survey the damage. The front of my small car was crushed almost beyond recognition. The tire had then rolled over the roof and made a sizeable dent in the back as well. Knowing that in Volkswagens the motor is in the rear, I attempted to open the back to assess the damage. Assess the damage? I had no idea what I was looking for. But no matter, because the latch on the back was well bent and would not yield to my attempts to open it.

I slid back into my car and once again gave in to tears of frustration. Now what? In the days before car phones, and on a fairly deserted highway with no houses in sight, what were my options? I contemplated walking for help, but to where? I had no idea where I would find a house. Two cars whooshed by with no apparent notice of me or my plight. Chilly now, I tried to coax the motor into starting. At least I could get some heat. But it protested loudly, spluttered and died again.

As I further contemplated my options, liking none of them, a police car miraculously appeared and pulled in behind me. I was sure it must be a mirage and closed my eyes, thinking it would be gone when I opened them. There was a tap at my window.

"Miss? Are you all right?" the concerned face was just discernable in the fading light. I rolled down the window with some difficulty and assured him that I was unhurt.

"I was just up the road," he told me. "A car that passed you told me you were in trouble. Come on into the cruiser and get warm." With teeth chattering, a combination of cold and shock, I gratefully complied.

On that cold March night, the officer who came to my aid was my guardian angel in disguise. After sitting with me in the cruiser until I was able to tearfully recount my story, he brought me to the station, saying that he would soon be off duty and would take me home.

"To Boston?" I asked incredulously, knowing that it would be close to a five-hour round trip for him. Maybe I should go to my parents', I thought, but he interrupted my calculations of distance.

"Sure," he said. "My sister lives there. I am overdue for a visit anyway."

It never crossed my naive mind that his offer was made in anything but good will. Nor should it, as his intentions were entirely honorable. I believe that he was just a kind and generous person.

After his shift, he took me out for dinner and drove me back home. My car was towed to a nearby garage, with a promise that he would have the mechanic call me on Monday to let me know the damage. My police officer friend would make several more trips to Boston after that night, and we would share several other dinners together until I decided that my guardian angel of that March night and I had little in common other than my harrowing experience. I recount this decision with some guilt, but I will always be thankful for his help nonetheless.

On Monday morning, I dragged myself sheepishly to the office, knowing that I had to announce that I was without a car and therefore out of commission for making visits. Herb did not look pleased as I told him. I was convinced that beneath his glower there was an "I told you so," but all he said when I had finished my tale was, "You should catch up on your dictation!"

For the next three weeks I was stranded in the office, borrowing my father's car when I could, while my insurance company, unable to locate the truck, tried to decide who was at fault. After pleas that their indecision was keeping me from doing my job and threats of changing companies, they finally concluded that the accident had been "an act of God" and paid to have my car repaired.

When I told Herb of the insurance company's ruling, he chuckled.

"Yeah, God got you for working on Saturday," he quipped.

What did I expect from an ex-priest?

Questions for Thought _____

1. Are you a person who likes to work overtime? What impact might working overtime have on your life?

2. How might you have reacted if your supervisor said that he was against something, but did not actually forbid you from doing it?

3. What might you have thought when you visited the O'Donnells? Would you have done anything about your feelings?

4. How do you react when the unexpected happens? What would you have done if your car had been disabled as this worker's was?

5. How do you know when a do-gooder means to help or when your safety is at risk?

13

Haunted by Echoes

It was close to a month before I had my car back. Today, the amount of damage would have caused an insurance company to call the car totaled, and the search for a new car might have held me up even longer. I was glad to have my little Bug back, not as good as new perhaps, but serviceable. By the time I was ready to be on the road again, I was caught up on my dictation (one of the few times in my career!), and had made as many telephone contacts as I could. The Ragusas were still doing well. Theresa kept me on the phone with her proud tales of all that Jerry could now do. Gabby had settled well into the Devers. Tara was her parents' pride even though her adoptive Mom had finally realized that she was pregnant. Technically, it was not up to me to check on the Van Dykes. It would be up to the Illinois agency that had first dealt with them. But feeling confined in the office and needing a boost, I chanced a call. Tom was again the parent at home. He made me feel that I was just the person he wanted to talk with, and babbled enthusiastically about Skipper and the rest of the family.

"He certainly can ask questions!" commented Tom, and I knew that Skipper had indeed settled in.

I also managed to find two couples for the babies that I had seen on the day of my accident, but I didn't want to call them until I knew that I could arrange the placement. So it was that my first week back on the road was spent in the pleasant task of placing two healthy babies with two enthusiastic couples, always an uplifting venture.

Herb said that he had another case for me, but could not find the file. The case, a three-year-old boy who had been severely sexually abused by his mother, had been referred to the Adoption Unit a year ago, but the petition to terminate parental rights had not been filed. Now the petition had been allowed, and we were ready to assess the child for possible placement. But the manila folder containing the child's record could not be found.

"How can a record just disappear?" I asked incredulously. "Now that I think of it, I can't find Jessica Barton's file, either!"

"Your guess is as good as mine. Have you done any dictation on the Barton file lately? Maybe it's in the secretarial pool. As for this new case, I am totally at a loss as to where it is. Keep your eyes open for it. In the meantime, I'll see if I can get a duplicate from the office that referred it to us."

When I first began at the office, files were kept in manila folders. A dropped file meant that you spent a bit of time trying to reorder the papers chronologically. A lost file meant a great deal of work at reconstructing what one could. Later, we began to use large green binders that were much more difficult to misplace, and the loose-leaf arrangements kept the pages more securely in order. Today, most information is kept in a computer-based file with a hard copy backup in the green binder, a much more efficient system. I spent the better part of that afternoon searching for the missing files with no success.

I had also spoken to Herb of my concerns about Mrs. O'Donnell. He had no answers either, and suggested that I make another visit as soon as I was able. But by the end of that week, we were told that we had another task.

"The building is going to be renovated," Herb told us in a unit meeting. "We are being moved into the Welfare office and they are going downstairs while our office is remodeled."

"Why don't they just move us and remodel instead of rearranging two offices?" asked Scott, my colleague who was always the rational one.

Herb shrugged. "Who knows. Probably because that would be the sensible way to do things. We don't ask, we just do what we're told! The joys of state service."

The next two weeks were spent organizing cases so that each worker would know where his or her cases were when the move was made. The other office workers had already been moved, so we also took time to survey our new work environment.

"This will be our unit," Herb toured us around the archaic building that we would occupy for the next year while renovations of our former office were accomplished.

"Ugh!" Deirdre wrinkled her nose. "It's filthy!"

"Yes, it is a bit," agreed Herb. "We were hoping the landlord would paint it, but he rationalizes that in a year it will be renovated anyway. So any cleaning will be up to us. If you think this is bad, wait until you see my office!"

We surveyed our potential area with distaste, and anxious to see something worse, followed Herb to his new office. He led us to a small cubicle that was once painted a very bright yellow. However, the once yellow walls were now a dull grayish tan. The only hint of the original color was visible where pictures had apparently been hung.

"What happened to this place?" exclaimed Samantha in disgust.

"The guy in this office smoked stogies—cigars," explained Herb. I was surprised that Herb, a cigarette smoker himself, apparently took a dim view of cigar smokers. But a look at the office made me tend to agree.

"A little detergent and a few sponges will improve this!" chirped Sam, always the positive and energetic one.

"You're kidding!" chimed Scott and Deirdre almost in unison. Scott added, "It's not in my job description!"

"Mine either," agreed Sam. "But we can't expect our poor supervisor to move into this mess." Deirdre looked skeptical.

"Sure, we can clean it up," Zach seemed to be won over by her idea. "Working together, we could get it done in a day."

Spurred on by Sam and Zach, we spent the next Friday in a cleaning party. By the end of the day, Herb's office was close to its original bright yellow, and our unit space looked ready for us to occupy.

"Don't think I'll fall asleep on the job!" commented Herb, as he gazed around his newly cleaned and very bright office. He was nonetheless pleased, and promised to take us all out to lunch as a token of his thanks. As I think of that cleaning party, I am warmed by feelings of nostalgia. Our mutual resolve to improve our new office gave us a sense of camaraderie that my later colleagues lacked. When we finally made our move, it was with pride and cooperation.

We had only been in our new office for a week, still trying to sort out the boxes and figure out what was where, when one of the workmen from the renovation project came over with an armful of papers.

"Found these behind the wall when we knocked it down," he said. "Anything important?" He dumped the papers unceremoniously on an empty desk.

"Where exactly were these?" asked the assistant director of our office as she perused the wrinkled remains. The pile on the desk would have excited the pornography shops down the street. For here was file after file of descriptive sexual abuse cases.

"Behind the wall on the East side of the building. There was a little hole between the wall and the sheetrock. Not sure how these could have gotten in there. Unless someone put them there!" the workman went off, shaking his head, convinced, I am sure, that the former inhabitants of the office he was renovating were a bit strange.

After exhaustive interviews, the administration finally pieced together what had happened. Apparently Gertie, our resident crusader for moral reform, had stuffed the files that she found particularly objectionable in a spot where she deemed they would do no further harm. In her distorted psyche, there appeared to be no room to consider the time and wasted energy that would have been expended to find the files. We watched expectantly as the secretary in question disappeared behind the closed door of the director. We hoped for her dismissal, or at least a severe chastisement. We never did know what happened, only that after an afternoon off, Gertie was back at her desk the next day. However, the typing schedule was changed so that each unit had its own specific secretary to do the typing. Gertie was not numbered among these, and I believe she spent the remainder of her days typing out forms.

It was almost three months before I was again able to visit the O'Donnells. I had called several times, and when I did find someone in, was assured by Bev or Warren O'Donnell that all was going well.

The flowers were in full bloom as I drove to the O'Donnell home. The sunlight was a welcome change after the week or so of rain that we just experienced. Therefore, I was quite surprised when I arrived at O'Donnell's to find that the shades were drawn at almost every window. I hardly recognized the obese woman who greeted me.

"Mrs. O'Donnell?" I asked, and immediately regretted it. It must have been obvious that I had noticed the change in her. But her round face registered little as she let me in.

"He's sick," she said quietly, without preamble. I assumed that she meant David, and expressed my concern.

"What's wrong?"

"I called the doctor," she began. "He said it was a flu or something."

"Did he see him," I asked. "Or put him on medication?"

She hesitated for a moment and then responded, "The doctor said that he'd call something in."

"Do you want me to pick it up for you?" I realized that she would hardly be able to leave the baby or take him with her if he was ill.

"No!" she almost barked at me and then in her usual tone, "No. Warren will pick it up."

Bev O'Donnell lowered herself into a chair that creaked beneath her weight.

"Let's let him sleep," she suggested quietly. "We'll just talk."

As we sat and made small talk, I began to feel terribly incompetent. There was something wrong here, I knew, but I had no idea what. I chided myself for not reading more. If I had had more schooling in psychology would I be able to figure out what was going on with this mother.

I left, never having seen David, and feeling as though I needed help on this case. I would ask Herb if we could bring the case before our consulting psychiatrist next week. In the meantime, I told Mrs. O'Donnell that I would call her the next day to see how David was doing. I again offered to pick up any medication that she might need, and was again politely refused.

As I drove home, I could not shake the feeling of impending doom. I had planned to stay with my parents, halfway between the O'Donnells' and Boston, but no sooner had I gotten in the door than I felt a need to call Herb. He agreed that things did not sound good with Mrs. O'Donnell, and suggested that we schedule an appointment for a psychiatric consultation the next afternoon rather than waiting a week.

The phone message awaiting me on my desk the next morning changed our plans considerably. "Please call Dr. Raymond Morris. Important."

I did not know a Dr. Morris, I thought, as I quickly dialed the number on the pink message paper. I was put on hold for a minute, and then connected with a deep male voice. After I identified myself, Dr. Morris began by asking if I was the worker who was supervising the adoption of David. When I said that I was, he told me that he was calling with permission from Warren O'Donnell.

"Mrs. O'Donnell and her son were both admitted to the hospital last night. Her son is severe failure to thrive, and Mrs. O'Donnell has been admitted to the psychiatric unit. I would prefer not to fill you in on the phone. How soon could you come out to the hospital to meet with me?"

I envisioned a day filled with appointments including the psychiatric consultant on just this case, but decided from the seriousness of his tone that everything could be postponed. I assured him that I could be out later that day.

Mid-afternoon found me seated in an office of the medical center listening to Dr. Morris' recounting of what seemed to me an almost unbelievable story. Dr. Morris met me outside his hospital office with the introduction: "I am the O'Donnells' family doctor. I am also on staff here at the hospital." He invited me into his roomy office and offered me a seat.

"What do you know of Mrs. O'Donnell's childhood?" asked the stocky, balding man, by way of preamble.

"We do talk with adoptive applicants a bit about their backgrounds," I told him. In fact, I had reviewed the O'Donnell's file before I left the office and was now glad that I had done so.

"I know that Mrs. O'Donnell was the middle of three children, has a brother who is ten years older and a sister two years younger. Her father died when she was seven, and her brother all but assumed her father's role. Her mother died several years ago, and she is not close to her brother. She sees her sister on some holidays, but does not consider her particularly close." I was pleased that my memory was serving me well.

The big doctor smiled, perhaps at my youthful need to prove that I was competent and well informed.

"At least we are on the same page," he said. "In fact, Mrs. O'Donnell was sexually abused by her father from about two years old until his death. His death was traumatic, first because Mrs. O'Donnell was with him when he died, and partly because her mother seems to have blamed her for his death. It was a tumor on the brain, nothing that could have been blamed on a child. But families can be cruel to one another," he said with some element of irony in his voice. He paused, as if reflecting on some hidden meaning of his statement in his own life. Apparently shaking the feeling, he rose and poured himself a cup of coffee from the coffee maker at one end of the office.

"Coffee?" I declined and he continued.

"Right after her father's death, Mrs. O'Donnell turned to her brother, who continued to sexually abuse her until the day she was married at twenty-one." He paused again, perhaps waiting for his words to sink in. But I was still confused. What did this have to do with what was happening now?

"Her sister, whose name is. . . ." he looked down at a file on his desk. "Jane Avery was also abused by the brother. We did not know any of this until this morning when Miss Avery arrived at the hospital. She calls periodically and just happened to call last night. Warren . . ." he stopped and looked at me. "Forgive me. Warren and I have been friends since childhood."

I nodded. His use of Warren's first name did not make me think any less of his professionalism.

"Warren had come home from a trip and felt that the baby, David, looked ill. He was concerned, and insisted that they take him to his pediatrician. As they were leaving, Jane Avery called, and Warren told her why they could not talk. The pediatrician had not seen him almost since they got David and was concerned. When he saw the child, he diagnosed him as failure to thrive, and hospitalized him immediately. He is still here if you need to see him."

"Will he be okay?" I asked. I thought to myself about Mrs. O'Donnell's explanation that the doctor had diagnosed the baby with the flu. What was behind her lie?

"Yes, we have him on an IV. It will take a while, but he can be built up. He may require tube feeding until he is ready to eat again on his own." As he spoke, I thought of adorable Billy, who had little resemblance to the child I was hearing about now. Then I remembered Beverly O'Donnell.

"But Mrs. O'Donnell?"

"Warren was furious when he found out what had happened to the baby. He accused Beverly of neglecting him, and there was a terrible scene in the waiting room. He stormed out, and she became hysterical." Having told me of his relationship with her husband, he now seemed comfortable calling Mrs. O'Donnell by her first name as well.

"The nurses calmed her down, but she was so upset that they were concerned that she would hurt herself. She kept saying that she wanted to die. She was convinced that she had killed her son and her husband had left her."

"The poor woman!" I said spontaneously. He glanced at me pensively.

"I have been in touch with Warren and he is with Beverly now. He feels terrible, and is more attentive than I have ever seen him. Warren is a good sort, but he is a workaholic and that comes first."

But I was still thinking about mother and child.

"Do you know what happened to the baby?" I asked.

When he began again, I wondered if he had heard my question.

"Anyway, when Jane Avery came here this morning, she filled in a bit of history. She had called the hospital after talking to Warren last night and discovered that her sister was admitted. She rushed here, feeling that we should know about their childhoods. I am glad she did." He poured himself another cup of coffee, and continued.

"Miss Avery said that she never married and was surprised when Beverly did. They had learned to hate men and not to trust them." He stopped, as if interrupted by an insight of his own.

"But then, Warren is away so frequently that she really doesn't have to deal with him much."

I suddenly thought about this woman whose childhood experiences had shown her men in abusive roles. Yes, it was amazing that she had married. I wondered if she was looking for someone to dispel the echoes of her past. Ironically, she had chosen Warren O'Donnell, a nice enough man, but one who I would never see as a warm and fuzzy person. Maybe she felt relief when he was away. Then I thought of David, her son . . . a miniature man . . . and a glimmer of understanding began to take shape.

"So David being a male," I began tentatively. Dr. Morris looked at me and I wondered if he was impressed by my new insight or had just concluded that I was awfully slow not to get the picture before.

"Until Beverly understands her feelings, I question how well she can give to a male child." The pronouncement seemed abrupt, and I was startled. Before I had a chance to consider the implications of his statement, he continued.

"But, there's another problem here. Beverly does care for David in her own distorted way. And Warren adores him. I know that you people have the ability to remove the baby from the home. The supervisory year is not up yet," he hesitated, looking at me for a reaction. It had never occurred to me that I had the power to take David out of this situation. Recognizing this responsibility, I felt overwhelmed by confusion.

"I hope that you will not take him, however." Dr. Morris' voice interrupted my confused thoughts. "I believe that this would be devastating for both Beverly and Warren. Beverly would feel like the ultimate failure, and I believe that it might destroy the marriage." If he thought that he had helped my comfort with a decision by his words, he was very wrong. I envisioned taking David when he was released from the hospital and saw a distraught couple watching me leave and convinced that I had destroyed their lives. Okay, I thought, I am out of my league here!

Morris was continuing. "I got the impression that Beverly's sister, Miss Avery, would be willing to stay with them for awhile, taking care of David when he is released. She is a nurse, so that I am confident that she could handle the situation. In the meantime, Beverly would receive regular therapy and Warren has agreed that they should also seek couple's counseling. I am hoping that this will be agreeable to the agency." The next move was obviously mine.

I considered the situation. In any family there may be problems. If David had been born to the O'Donnells, this might still have happened. Fleetingly, I remembered the O'Donnell's file that said that they had a fertility problem of unknown origin. I wondered if this inability to conceive children was in fact related to Mrs. O'Donnell's past.

Dr. Morris was apparently waiting. I looked up and his face was drawn. He looked tired, and I wondered how much he had invested in this couple that he had known for so long.

"The decision is not mine entirely," I began. "I will have to discuss it with my supervisor. The plan sounds workable, and if you feel that they do want David, I would hate to uproot him again." We agreed that I would get back to him.

"Beverly is sedated right now, but if you would like to see David, I will take you to him," he told me.

David's bed was in a room on the pediatric ward. There were two beds, but one was empty. As we entered the room, I realized that the figure that I saw huddled by the bedside was Warren O'Donnell. He looked smaller than I remembered him. His face was streaked with tears and I was surprised at how vulnerable he looked.

"I'm sorry," he mumbled when he saw me. "I'm so, so sorry. I always wanted a son. He was perfect." And he began to sob. Morris put an arm around his shoulder and he seemed to gain his composure.

"It's okay, Warren. It's okay."

I looked away from the two men to the small figure in the hospital crib. He was sleeping with the lines from an IV emerging from beneath a bandage on his arm. David, who I had once known as healthy adorable Billy, was pale and emaciated. I knew that failure to thrive meant that the baby had slipped below the fifth percentile in weight expected for his age, but after almost six months in placement, he looked hardly bigger than he had on the day I first saw him. His eyes fluttered briefly, and he opened then. He looked at me and then at his father huddled with Dr. Morris. As if finding nothing to keep him awake, his eyes closed and he returned to the peacefulness of sleep.

"He'll get his energy back as the IV begins to build him up," Dr. Morris whispered, as if to reassure both Warren and me.

I left the two men there with sleeping David as I returned to my car and started the long drive back to the office. I was scheduled to meet Herb on this case as soon as I returned, but looking at my watch decided that I had better call him. It was almost closing time, and I was sure that he would be worried.

As always, Herb was supportive.

"Well you certainly have gotten a trial by fire," he mused. He agreed that it would not be wise to remove David, provided all the plans suggested by Dr. Morris could be put into place.

In the years to come, I would learn that removals of children from placement are never easy. It is a myth perpetrated by both insecure couples and the public that adoption agencies will remove children from adoptive homes for the slightest reason. This is certainly not true. Over the years I have held the hand of an adoptive mother undergoing chemotherapy, supported a couple seeking divorce but still wanting to keep their adopted child, and mourned with an adoptive father whose wife died suddenly, helping him then to make arrangements for the care of their adopted son. Removals are more often at the request of a couple than by the decision of an agency. Like any relationship, an adoption requires a mutually satisfying chemistry and an emotional balance among all the individuals. When these are not achieved, a placement may fail. Removing a child is not what anyone hopes for, but such things do happen.

For the O'Donnells, however, it seemed that what was needed was support and understanding, and that is what we had agreed to offer.

Questions for Thought _____

1. How would being out of commission have affected you? How might you have reacted?

2. What do you think of the work party? Would you have participated in such an event?

3. What was your reaction to the records behind the wall? Does it alter your impressions of Gertie?

4. How would you have handled the interview with Mrs. O'Donnell? What would your gut have been telling you?

5. How would you have handled the O'Donnell case? What are your feelings about what happened?

6. What feelings must have been going on for Warren O'Donnell?

7. What effects do you think this situation might have on little David?

8. Do you think the final plan was a good one? Why or why not?

14

Old Rewards and New Challenges

Spring, with its promise of new birth and healing, gave way to summer. I visited the O'Donnell's every few weeks. Jane Avery had taken a leave of absence to help her sister, and I watched as their relationship blossomed. So often, survivors of abusive situations are never able to talk with their siblings about the horror that each endured. But as Beverly O'Donnell continued in therapy, she and her sister shared more and more of their lives and feelings with one another. Capable of the warmth that was difficult for her sister, Jane Avery also modeled mothering as she cared for David, who began to look more like the little Billy I had first known. Warren managed to change positions at work, insuring that he was home more. I guessed that the marriage counseling that the couple had agreed to attend was a challenge for both of them, but they persevered.

Although I doubted that the O'Donnell home ever became idyllic, it seemed to be functioning well enough to allow Jane Avery to return to work in early September. In her wake, she had left a stronger Beverly and a relationship that would enrich both her life and her sister's for years to come. Our agency extended the supervisory year for about six months, but finally felt comfortable in allowing the adoption to be legalized. By that time, David was an active toddler, devoted to his father. His still quiet mother watched their relationship flourish with more peace than she once might have done. She had become a relatively competent, if not overly demonstrative mother, had lost considerable weight, and seemed much more sure of herself. I was thankful for a caring doctor and a competent sister who seemed to have made it possible.

As I watched the fall and then the winter holidays come and go, I realized how much I enjoyed this work. The long hours, the confusion, and the travel were all rewarded by the radiant faces of couples as they held their newly placed child in their arms. It was decidedly the positive side of social work.

January and February brought with them the finalization of my first adoption placements. The Devers were the first on the court docket. They appeared at the courthouse on the appointed day, looking like the perfect family. The boys, dressed in suits and ties mirroring their always well-dressed father, ushered in a ruffle-clad Gabby, all smiles and dozens of new freckles. Jeannine, ever in charge with her quiet, competent manner, had invited the Polinskis, an unprecedented move, but one that showed her innate kindness. But Herman Polinski had died the week before and his widow, grieving, did not feel up to being part of the ceremony, having lost her lifelong companion. Perhaps too, the court hearing was the event that marked the culmination of her loss of her little Gabby. She had been accepting of the Devers and had been included by them as a surrogate grandparent, but I was sure that it was not the same for the older woman who had already lost her own child by birth.

Gabby seemed totally unaware of the multiple emotions that surrounded her, so involved was she in her new home and the meaning of this appearance before the judge who would pronounce her legally a Dever. We all waited, some more patiently than others, in the hall outside the judge's chambers, expectant of the call that would say that we were next. When it did come, the two little Devers and the one soon-to-be Dever became model children and marched solemnly into the spacious office, sitting quietly by their parents in anticipation of further instructions. The judge who soon emerged from some unknown location must have been impressed by the attractive family before him. What a pleasant change from his other duties of the day. He smiled broadly, joked with the children, and asked Gabby if this was indeed what she wanted. With newfound poise and a good deal of awe in the face of this black-garbed figure, Gabby looked at both of her parents, smiled and said that it was. And with the rap of a gavel, Gabrielle Jean Dever was legally born.

The Devers invited me back to their home for an adoption party, the first of many that I would attend over the years. These parties have always been a high point of adoption work. They commemorate not only a new life for parents and children, but a successful matching and placement for the adoption worker. The Ragusas' party several weeks later was probably the best attended of any I experienced. Their large apartment seemed small when crammed with a multitude of relatives and friends. I vowed that I would never eat again after partaking of the room full of goodies that must have been a combined effort of a variety of donors. Otherwise, it would have taken Theresa at least a month to amass the feast that was presented. Jerry looked wonderful, toddling about in a cute little sailor suit that Theresa had made for the occasion. Next to Jerry, I was treated as the most important person at the affair. Theresa continued to introduce me as the "wonderful lady who brought me my bambino," and I admit to a feeling of pride. When the couple returned two years later to adopt another baby, I hoped that their new placement worker appreciated their warm enthusiasm as much as I did.

The Tylers' adoption date had to be postponed slightly as Alexis recuperated from a difficult delivery. But on the appointed date, the Tylers, Tara, and baby Will appeared with smiling faces to become one legal family. They even managed a small, somewhat quiet party despite the adoptive mother having a new baby. As promised, I quietly sent a note to Tara's birth mother, April, assuring her that her baby with the lovely name was in good hands and legally adopted. She had indeed gone to college, and I was sure was continuing to make beautiful music.

It was important to have these moments of cheer amidst the ever-present challenges of still searching for homes for children like Skipper's sister Franny, or Jessica Barton. And I worried about the O'Donnells and the effects of David's failure to thrive. But at least in the latter case, all seemed to be well.

I received a brief note from Laura Van Dyke when Skipper's adoption was finalized, and I so wished I could have been there. By spring there were other finalizations, and it felt good to know that my work had made a difference in the lives of these couples and children.

I had been with the agency for several years when Herb suggested that I might enjoy a new challenge. After numerous delays, we had finally been installed in our new offices, had witnessed the renovation of the old, and were pleased that we now had a large conference room. When couples applied for adoption, they were invited to a large group meeting to let them know what type of children were available and the next step they should follow. We had always borrowed space from another office to hold these, but now we would be able to hold them in or own spacious conference room.

"You might like to sit in on an informational meeting," Herb suggested. Was I being groomed for the homefinder position that would soon be vacated, I wondered with excitement. Most people who were hired by the agency came in as placement workers, as I had. Eventually, it was possible to become a homefinder, those workers who studied applicants to be potential adoptive couples. I thought that I might enjoy this role, but since there had not been any positions vacant since I was hired, I had never considered it.

"And maybe you would like to try a group homestudy," Herb continued. "With Janet leaving, Claire will need someone to co-lead with her. Interested?"

Interested! I sure was, and flattered to be asked. Homefinding had always seemed like the essence of adoption to me. It was important that children were placed, but having enough appropriate couples to receive these children was vital.

Most agencies at that time studied couples alone, conducting several interviews to get to know the couple and acquaint them with the important issues in adoption. More recently, our agency had begun to see couples in groups of five or six. Not only was it possible to see more couples in a given time period, but the peer interaction allowed people to feel more comfortable and might spark in them questions that would not occur to them if seen with only their spouse. After the groups were completed, couples were seen in their homes to get to know both home environment and the other children who lived there. Training couples to be skillful adoptive parents and having the intuition to know when applicants' issues would prevent them from a positive adjustment to adoption was an art that some workers did not possess. Claire was a competent homefinder and I would enjoy working with her.

"Of course, you will just be helping out at the moment," Herb must have recognized that my bubble was growing a bit prematurely. "Janet's pregnancy has meant that she cannot see as many couples and she will be leaving soon. We need someone to do groups so we don't get backed up. But you will still have to do your placements. How is little Gavin coming?"

I had been working with Gavin, the baby addicted to heroin at birth, for some time. His first foster mother had been overwhelmed by the constant irritable crying that was typical of many such babies. We had moved the baby several times, until a new foster mother, a nurse, had taken him into her home and her heart.

"It looks like the foster mom might be interested in adopting him," I said. "After all he's been through, I think that would be the best for him." I liked Gavin's current foster mother. She had a way with the fussy and often ill child that spoke of a special relationship between them.

"That sounds great," responded Herb, only half listening. I knew that he had confidence in my intuitive ability to discern what was best for my clients. It made me feel good.

"So, if I am doing a group with Claire, maybe I can also do an assessment on this foster home as a potential adoptive home. What do you think?" The more home-finding experience I could get before the position became open, the better, I reasoned.

"Before you get too caught up in a foster home adoption or your new homefind-ing tasks, I have another placement case for you." He went off to produce the promised file. I recognized Herb's technique, and marveled at how well he had come to know me. When I got excited about an idea, I tended to throw myself into it with enthusiasm, not always looking before I leaped. This was not the first time that Herb had said, in his own way, try it out before you decide!

He presented me with a file saying, "Here's an interagency case for you. Have fun."

I read over the case and discovered that we had just approved a young Black couple but had no Black children at that time. It would be my job to go through the adoption exchange, similar as I had with Skipper, find a child that met their needs in another agency and arrange the placement with the other agency's worker. I suspected that I would not have to look out-of-state for this child, and very soon I had found what seemed like an appropriate candidate in the Massachusetts adoption exchange manual. The agency was a small, private one, and I hoped that they were also looking for a couple like the Walters. A quick call to the other agency satisfied me that the placement might become a reality. The worker, an older woman by the sound of her voice, agreed that I would talk with the couple and set a tentative date for them to meet the baby.

"Hi," greeted a pleasant voice with a soft southern drawl, as I was hanging up the phone from the call. "I hear that Herb has volunteered you to help me out with my new group. That's great."

I looked up to see Claire Christianson standing in front of my desk. From Savannah, Georgia, Claire took a good deal of ribbing about her southern accent. But she was a good sport about it, and well liked. She was also respected as the best home-finder in the office.

"Come on," she said. "I have some applications. We can choose a group now if you have a minute."

"Sure, just one quick call first," I agreed, hoping she didn't think I was any less interested. But I did want to line up this placement.

Michelle Walters was delighted that I called.

"Martin and I thought there would be a long wait," she confided. "Martin is home this morning. He's on the night shift. Can I put him on the other line so we can both hear about the baby?"

After a brief pause and voices in the background, Martin Walters picked up the extension. I told the couple what I knew of the baby, and we arranged to meet briefly in my office for me to tell them more of what I knew. Then, if they wanted to proceed, we would meet at the other agency to hear more about him, and the worker would arrange for them to see the baby. Mission accomplished! And I went off in search of Claire.

Choosing couples for a group was a combination of skill, intuition and a lot of guess work, I would learn. It took us several hours, lunch, and quite a few laughs to choose what we assumed would be a workable group. The couples we had not chosen would be either seen individually when a homefinder's schedule allowed it, or picked up for a later group.

"Great," said Claire when she closed the last file. "I think we'll make a great team!"

I left the meeting feeling warm and accomplished, sure that nothing could go wrong.

Questions for Thought

1. What do you feel were the pros and cons of the arrangement with the O'Donnells?

2. What would have been your feelings about the finalization of your first cases?

3. How do you react to new challenges? Do you jump right in or tend to be more tentative?

4. What might go into choosing potential adoptive couples for a successful group?

15

Expecting the Unexpected

I reread the directions in front of me in utter frustration. I certainly hoped that I gave better directions that the other agency's worker had given me. Here I was, stopped at a light I suspected of being one I had seen at least three times before, in an unknown city, and I was lost. How hard could this agency be to find? I was well aware that small, private agencies were often housed in what was once a private home, often in a residential part of the city, but could it really be that difficult to locate? I finally resigned myself to defeat and called the agency to ask where I had gone wrong only to discover that a left turn, which was supposed to be a right, had been part of the problem. I grumbled inwardly, sure that I had copied down the directions the way that Magdalene Parks, the social worker, had given them to me.

After finally finding the agency, I breathlessly explained who I was to the receptionist and was ushered into an office. I was greeted by a bespectacled Magdalene, who, being the source of the erroneous directions, I disliked immediately. She had the officious manner of someone who knows that she is right and could not be convinced otherwise. She was obviously annoyed that I was late and made no attempt to cover the fact.

"We decided to start without you!" she said in her stern, old schoolmarm voice. I decided to ignore her manner and looked beyond her at the couple that I had liked during our brief conversation. If a very dark complected woman can be called pale, that is how I would have described Michelle Walters. She sat, wringing a Kleenex in one hand with her concerned husband by her side. His face was shiny with perspiration. Whatever was happening?

Trying to figure out how I could find out what had caused my clients to look so dismayed, I asked, "Could you fill me in on what you have covered so far?"

"Well," huffed Magdalene. "I had told the Walters about little Franklin and his unfortunate birth. I hadn't expected to say it twice."

The picture was beginning to become clearer. Unfortunate birth? Not the terms I would have used. Sorry that I had to put the couple through whatever had upset them again, I nevertheless said, "I wish you could repeat it for my benefit."

Not the answer that Magdalene wanted perhaps, but that was tough!

"Franklin is a three-week-old baby who has been in foster care since birth. His mother was a Nigerian foreign student who was here for a year. She is of excellent parentage, five feet, four inches tall, dark complexion, brown eyes, and black hair. She is healthy, or was."

"Was?" I interrupted. Magdalene was not pleased, but went on.

"One night when she was coming home from a school dance, she was brutally raped." I noticed Michelle Walters react as if she had been hit by each of the last two words. Magdalene seemed not to notice.

"He was a Black man whom she believes was about 6 feet tall. Nothing else is known about him. Franklin had a normal delivery and is healthy. His maternal grandparents," Magdalene's words faded off as I watched Mrs. Walters. There were small tears in the corners of her large brown eyes.

"Are there any other questions?" Magdalene finished. I looked at the Walters, who seemed in need of an advocate.

"Actually, I wonder if the Walters and I might talk privately," I said. I was surprised at my own tone that seemed to imply that this was not a request but an insistence.

No sooner had Magdalene left the room, when Michelle Walters burst into tears.

"I'm sorry, Martin. I am so sorry. I just can't take him. I would look at him everyday and know that," Martin Walters knelt down to comfort his wife.

"It's okay, Mickey. There'll be another baby." Then he looked at her plaintively and then at me.

"I'm sorry, too," he began. "But my wife was . . ." he knew that he need not continue. Our eyes met and he must have known that I understood. Undoubtedly, his wife had also been raped, perhaps in her school days, and this would serve as a constant reminder. Whatever had possessed this insensitive social worker to tell this couple the brutal facts? Surely they could have been avoided so that baby Franklin could have had the benefit of the loving home that the Walters could provide. It was common to tell couples a bit about their potential child, but never anything that would prevent them from bonding. Professionalism prevented me from telling this couple what I thought of this social worker and her insensitivity, but I think that they knew.

"I don't believe that this baby is the one for you," I said, feebly hoping that they would not feel that this was their failure. "I am sure that we can find another."

On my ride back to the agency, I felt compassion for the young couple. After they left, I had told Magdalene that I did not feel that she should have been quite as blunt with her background information, only to be met with her haughty reply that it was the agency's policy to tell the couple all the facts. I have worked harmoniously with many private agencies since that day, and have never, to my relief, met another Magdalene Parks, nor have I had another negative experience.

Soon after this meeting, the Walters withdrew their application to adopt. Although private adoptions (when a couple finds a mother willing to release her baby directly to them) were not entirely legal at that time, I could not help but hope that the Walters found another way to have the baby that they so desperately wanted.

The Walters were still very much on my mind when Claire and I began our group. We had chosen the Wongs, the Nobles, the Donahues, the Moronis and the Coughlins to comprise our group. In the sessions, each two hours long and a week apart for five weeks, we discussed such topics as how children became available for adoption (dispelling the myth that birth parents have fallen from the face of the earth), how they will expect to parent, their reasons for wanting to adopt, and their hopes and fears. Included in their interest in adoption as well was a discussion on their own infertility, if that was indeed the case. Most couples find this topic especially difficult. The ability to conceive children is something we take for granted in our culture. An inability to do so feels to many like the ultimate failure. Many men especially, as they buy into their need to be virile, see infertility as a stigma. Adoption homefinders learn to tread gently around this topic, being sensitive to the feelings of all concerned, both the infertile and their grieving but concerned partners.

Claire and I were discussing this topic during our third group meeting with this group. We had gotten to know a lot about them. The Wongs were a quiet second-generation Chinese couple who listened respectfully but said little. I was especially fond of Bricker and Ruby Noble, a warm and friendly Black couple who reminded me a bit of the Walters. They had one son of five and were anxious to adopt a girl. The Coughlins' relationship might have reminded me of the Polinskis, Gabby's foster parents, had it not been for their age and the fact that they had only been married a short time. Mrs. Coughlin was as wide as her husband was tall, but she was undaunted by the difference in height. Like Mrs. Polinski, she always had the last word, and meek Mr. Coughlin, just acquiesced with a "yes dear." But even in her most controlling moods, Mrs. Coughlin was likeable.

The Moronis had come in on the recommendation of Theresa Ragusa, who was Mr. Moroni's first cousin. Not as vivacious as Theresa, they were nonetheless enthusiastic and positive. The only couple that concerned us were the Donahues, or rather, Mr. Donahue. He was the kind of man that I personally disliked but I tried not to let this color my opinion of his suitability as an adoptive father. He seemed to have dedicated himself to being as macho as possible. He was Mr. Sportsman and he frequently attempted to engage the men in an aside about some football or baseball issue. He bragged about everything, from their huge house to his poker prowess to the fact that he still had a full head of hair and was the only male in the group not showing the evidence of age in a thinning dome or receding hairline. Mrs. Donahue looked embarrassed when her husband began one of his tangents, but obviously had learned not to intervene.

We knew that the discussion of fertility would be difficult, so Claire and I reviewed the couples' medical records before we met with them. All of the couples had some type of fertility issue. This was not always the case. Many couples chose to adopt for other reasons than their own inability to conceive. And for many, like the Tylers or the O'Donnells, the reasons that they had not yet conceived was not clear or obvious from medical exams.

As we looked over the files, we noted that Sue Wong, Debbie Moroni, and Agnes Coughlin all had medical problems that made it difficult or impossible for them to conceive. Soon after the birth of their son, Bricker Noble had contracted the mumps, which had made him sterile.

"Will you look at this!" Claire exclaimed, as she reviewed the Donahue's file. "Explains why Mr. Big's got a chip on his little ole shoulder!"

I laughed, not at the content but at Claire's engaging style. I read over her shoulder that Patrick Donahue had a condition that made it difficult for him to impregnate his wife.

"Doctor friend of mine used to call it 'lazy sperm'," Claire explained. "The sperm move so slowly that it's tough for them to get where they're going."

I found myself a bit embarrassed by her candor. The times were not as conducive to the frank discussion of sexuality as they are now. I had been sheltered at home, and at twenty-four was not used to discussing sexual issues openly. I had better get used to it if I intended to work with infertile couples, I concluded.

"Let's see if this tapers his sail," said my coworker, who admitted to being fed up by Donahue's monopolizing the group with his various unrelated discussions.

If we thought that the discussion of his infertility would in any way inhibit Patrick Donahue, we were much mistaken. Instead, he launched into the topic with his usual gusto and his characteristic lack of sensitivity. In great detail, he began to explain the remedies he had tried to solve his problem.

"The doctor said to use heat to get the little buggers moving," Donahue explained, while several of the others in the room began to fidget, slightly unsure where this was leading. As his explanation became more detailed, Sue Wong coughed and Debbie Moroni searched in her purse for something, anything that would keep her from having to be part of the discussion.

I could see Claire assessing the reactions of Mr. Donahue's peers. Claudia Donahue looked as though she would like nothing better than to disappear. All of the women would probably have wished they could join her while their husbands' reactions ranged from disinterest to disgust. I could tell that she was about to intervene when Bricker Noble spoke up. He was looking down as he quietly said.

"You know, Pat, I am not sure that the intimate details of your fertility problem benefit any of us. It seems to me that it's how you feel about it that counts. Even though we have our son, Adam, I was totally bummed out when I found out that I couldn't father any more kids. I felt like I had let Ruby down." He turned and looked straight at Patrick Donahue.

"How did you feel?" asked Bricker Noble pointedly. Bless you, Mr. Noble, I thought. I knew that I should be more empathetic. It was obvious that Mr. Donahue had a problem, but his affect had gotten to me, too.

Silence. Patrick Donahue was totally disarmed and obviously at a loss for words for the first time that I ever remembered. Claire let several moments pass, and then said softly.

"Sometimes it is difficult to talk about our feelings. Not being able to conceive a child is something that can seem especially hurtful. How does it feel?" Instead of looking at Mr. Donahue, she directed the comment to the whole group. There were tears in several eyes. She had taken the pressure off Donahue and at first I wondered why. Then I realized that his façade of bravado covered a very fragile ego that now was feeling shaky. I admired how Claire had handled the situation.

As the couples began to share what it had been like when they discovered they had fertility problems, I watched Patrick Donahue. He had been looking for attention, for acceptance, and now the well-timed words of Bricker Noble had let him know that he was not succeeding. Claudia Donahue watched her husband too, and finally, as if mustering her courage, she said, "I never told Patrick this, but at first, when we found out that he . . ." she glanced quickly at him, "We might have difficulty getting pregnant, I was angry. I had wanted a baby so much. It didn't seem fair. But when I realized how hurt Pat was," she stopped, gauging his reaction. He looked at his hands in his lap and said nothing.

"Then I realized that we should mean more to each other than our ability to have a baby. When he agreed to come here, I thought he felt the same way." Were her words a chastisement for his inappropriateness or a question about his motivation? It was difficult to tell. Mrs. Donahue stopped speaking, and Claire let the silence linger as if to bring home the point.

When the meeting ended, Patrick Donahue had still said nothing. It was as though he had been silenced and now could not find his voice. Robbed of his jokes and his bragging, he seemed to have nothing left.

"Phew," breathed Claire as we collected our papers after the couples had gone. "That was some meeting!"

"What do you think will happen?" I asked, knowing that couples being able to discuss their issues was an important part of the process.

"Not sure they're going to make it," answered Claire. "I just have a feeling."

"Will we have to refuse to place with them?"

Claire was thoughtful for a moment.

"I am not sure it will come to that," she said mysteriously. I would eventually learn how perceptive this woman could be when it came to judging people.

The next two meetings of our group went fairly smoothly. Patrick Donahue said little, but his wife seemed to have found her voice. There was a noticeable difference between them, however. Claudia seemed much less leery of her husband and more able to express herself.

When the meetings were completed, it was time to schedule home visits. Normally, each worker would take half of the couples but since I had never made a home visit, Claire suggested that I accompany her on one and then take one more to do on my own. She suggested that we go together to the Moronis' and that I visit the Nobles' by myself. We both recognized that they were probably the healthiest and most suitable couples for positive adoption.

"The Wongs are great, too," Claire told me. "But there are some cultural considerations there, and we should start you on an easier case." I already knew a bit about the couple's home and family life, deeply imbedded in the culture of Chinatown, and decided that I had a bit more to learn before I could assess their home effectively.

Our visit to the Moronis, as expected, went well. Like her cousin Theresa, Debbie Moroni wanted to feed us well. We left feeling that any child placed with this couple would be not only much loved, but well fed. I was anxious to make my visit to the Nobles. I liked both Bricker and his wife, Ruby, and looked forward to meeting their son, Adam. We talked easily as we sat in their living room. They lived in an attractive split level in a suburb of Boston. The finished basement served as a family room and overflow bedroom. The three bedrooms on the upper level allowed for Adam to still have his space while the new child would also have a room of her own. As we toured the house, I caught glimpses of five-year-old Adam, but he never seemed to stay long in the room we were in.

When we finished talking about the house, we settled in the living room while Ruby brought out some soda and cookies. I would really have a weight problem if I continued these visits, I mused. Still there was no Adam. Bricker talked about how excited they were to be adopting.

"Ruby has been so nervous," he smiled at her affectionately.

"I'll say," she admitted. "I don't know what I expected, but I sure was nervous about your visit. Poor Adam, I must have changed his clothes four times!"

"Speaking of Adam," Bricker began, "Where did he get to?"

"He's nervous too," his wife told him. "He's downstairs with his dog." She went to the basement stairs and called to her son. "Adam, come on up and meet the lady."

There was a muffled response from the basement.

"Aw, honey, come on," begged Ruby. More muffled replies. "Come to the bottom to the stairs, honey, so I can hear you."

"I can't come up." Came a child's voice from the bowels of the basement.

"But why?" Ruby sat on the steps and was almost pleading with him.

" 'Cause!" came the reply.

"Adam?" his father got into the act, gentle but firm. "Why won't you come up?"

" 'Cause!!" repeated the voice with more emphasis. " 'Cause, if you think I'm going to blow this whole thing, you're crazy!"

"Oh, poor Adam!" Ruby exclaimed. "I have really done a job on him with my nervousness!" and she disappeared down the stairs. After several moments of whispered conversation, mother and son emerged. She had apparently convinced him that he did not have it in his power to totally destroy their chance to adopt a baby sister. Adam was a delightful little boy who had been well prepared, despite his own fears that he might negatively influence the outcome of the home study. I left feeling that some little girl would be very lucky to have these folks for her new family.

Back at the office, Claire greeted me with enthusiasm.

"How'd it go? Good?" she asked. I gave her my assessment of the Nobles and asked how she had fared.

"The Coughlins and the Wongs are solid," she told me. "But a bit of unexpected news at the Donahues."

"What?" I couldn't imagine what new turn this case could have taken.

"They have withdrawn their application," Claire told me. "Claudia wants to separate."

"You're kidding!" This was something I had not expected.

"I guess the meetings brought up a lot of issues that have been going on for a long time," Claire continued. "Patrick just couldn't face his feelings, and Claudia suspects that he has been seeing someone."

"Ouch! That must have been a blow for her!" I felt badly for Claudia Donahue, who seemed to have tried so hard to please her husband until he had just pushed her too far.

"Actually, she is taking it pretty well," Claire said. "I think this may have given her an excuse to act. So many couples with shaky marriages think that having kids will bring them closer. It doesn't work that way! I think that she has really found a bit of herself in all this."

What a strange turn of events, I thought, wondering how Patrick Donahue would fare if he had begun another relationship. I wished Claudia well and hoped that someday she would be in a position to have the child that she craved.

I had enjoyed doing the group and told Claire that I would love to do others. Although I did do several other groups with her, Janet's unexpected decision to return after her maternity leave meant that I never was able to become a homefinder. But the groups gave me the best of both worlds, experience in some aspects of homefinding as well as in placement. My real joy came when a new child on my caseload proved to be the perfect match for the Nobles. Thus, I was able to continue my relationship with Ruby, Bricker, and Adam for another year until they too came before the court for their finalization of the adoption of thirteen-month-old Tasha Marie. Theirs was an adoption party that I especially enjoyed, as I got to see a couple who had first come to the agency nervous and expectant realize their dream of another child. It was a gift.

Questions for Thought

1. How would you have reacted if faced with a situation like the Walters interview at the other agency? How might you have handled the situation?

2. How much should adoptive couples be told about the circumstances around a child's birth? Why? What is the importance of this information?

3. How do you feel about the Walters' reaction? Would you have placed another baby with them had they not withdrawn their application?

4. What do you feel motivated the Walters to withdraw their application?

5. How might you have handled the situation with Mr. Donahue?

6. What was your impression of the Nobles? What feelings may have been going on in little Adam's head? How might you have handled it?

16

Graduate School and Beyond

What first gave me the idea to go to graduate school in social work? No more than an average student at the undergraduate level, I could not believe that I would actually consider putting myself through two more years of study. Was it Herb's tales of his graduate school career that had whetted my appetite for advanced study? Or was it my frustration when I realized that more knowledge when faced with cases like the O'Donnells might have given me more insight into their problems? Whatever spurred me on to apply to three graduate schools and eventually choose one continued to motivate me until I emerged two years later with a Master's in Social Work.

It was time to move on when I prepared to leave for my first year of graduate school. There were many reasons for this. Although I loved adoption work, I craved more knowledge. The Department was also offering a stipend to encourage their employees to better educate themselves. Provided I was willing to continue in any part of the State Department of Social Services for two years after I graduated, they would furnish me with a stipend that could cover my tuition and living expenses. Not a bad deal. I was also beginning to realize that my feelings about Herb had somewhere and somehow transformed from those one might feel toward an excellent supervisor to something more. As he encouraged me to enroll in graduate school and helped me find an apartment in the city where, he too, had gone to school, I realized that his feelings toward me had also altered. Once I was no longer his supervisee, we began a long and usually satisfying dating relationship that lasted several years until we parted, still friends.

Graduate school was quite different from my undergraduate experience. As an undergraduate, I had been right out of high school, dependent on my parents and not very serious about learning. Now, in graduate school, I found myself involved and dedicated to learning more about my chosen field. The classes meant something to me, as English 101 and Algebra never had. Here I was learning about real people and actual services. I could see the faces of my former clients as I read about the various issues that impeded people's ability to find happiness. I saw Mrs. O'Donnell as I studied about the residual effects of sexual abuse. I could imagine children like Skipper

95

and Gabby as I explored how separation affects children. Little Gavin, addicted to drugs at birth, stared out at me from the pages of a book on drugs and children. In every text and in every theory, a face jumped out at me. It seemed like an exciting adventure into understanding. I loved diagnosing problems and formulating treatment plans.

During my first year, I attended classes three days a week and spent the remaining two days in placement at an agency specializing in protective services. Another excellent supervisor and a challenging caseload sparked my interest in abused and neglected children. I also became involved in a program where I counseled a drug addict in a local house of correction. My second year, classes took up two days and placement in a child guidance clinic filled the other three. I learned there that I hated being confined to an office, and missed the field work that I had done in both adoption and my placement in the protective services division. Although I developed some excellent contacts for the future, I longed to return to visiting homes and other agencies.

Although the first year I lived alone in an apartment that Herb had helped me find, I was glad to move in with a newly found friend, Rachael, during my second year. I had always been interested in Judaism, from discussions with my Jewish friend in college to studying Jewish thought as a religion major. Rachael had grown up in a Jewish family but knew little of her heritage. Together we discovered much about Judaism and about our individual diversities. These were lessons that would serve me well in my later years in social work.

Rachael and I became involved in a group thesis with several other students. We were interested in the effects of recidivism in drug addiction. Through our field research in a major medical center in the area of our graduate school, we learned a great deal about addictive substances and the people who used them. I was to think back on this research many times during my years in protective services work as I watched addicted mothers attempt to care for their children or babies addicted at birth, going through the painful withdrawal that was brought upon them by their mother's habit. I cannot say that the research was brilliant, but the lessons learned from those we researched was invaluable.

My graduation with a master's degree in hand was an event that my parents had long hoped for. My father, with several advanced degrees of his own, had not dared to hope after my less-than-sterling performance as an undergraduate, that I would return for graduate school. Now he was about to burst his buttons as he watched me walk down the aisle to graduate. He was also convinced that I would eventually go on for a doctorate, a possibility that seemed totally out of the question to me. When I eventually received my doctorate several years after my father's death, I was glad that he had at least seen me get my Master's.

Armed with a degree, I had to decide my future. I owed the State of Massachusetts at least two years of service, a fact that I looked forward to rather than dreaded as some of my colleagues did. But where to do that service was the question. I had continued to work in adoption during the summers between my years in graduate school, but the fact that I was dating Herb made things somewhat awkward. Few people knew of our relationship, and we liked it that way. But, as a result, we had begun to feel somewhat clandestine in our relationship, which was both annoying and somehow exciting. Nevertheless, I decided that it might be better if I moved on, since the position of Assistant Director looked as if it might well be within Herb's grasp.

Since I had enjoyed my graduate school placement in protective services, I decided to apply for a transfer to the office where I had originally interviewed. Reg Forrester was still the Director and greeted me with enthusiasm.

"You've decided to check out the real world after a vacation in adoption, huh?" he asked with a chuckle. Little did I know how accurate this statement would be.

I was originally assigned to an ongoing unit, a group of workers who provided case management for cases that had already been determined to be abuse and neglect. Some children were still at home and it was our job to work with the parents to try to keep them there but also to insure their safety. Other children were in foster homes, and in addition to seeing them there, it would be my role to help the parents to mobilize their resources so that the children could be returned to them. If it seemed that these parents were still unable to care for their children, it would be up to me, as a worker in the ongoing unit, to refer them to the adoption unit.

Another worker had recently left, so I was to inherit many of her cases. I would soon learn that life in protective services was stressful and could be unrewarding. It was not unusual for workers to leave as they burned out on living day to day with the misery and maltreatment of children. The turnover in most protective services offices is quite high, which might account for the public's accusation that there is inconsistency in the way that cases are handled. After all, everyone has a different style of working, and with a new worker every few years, it is certainly possible for cases to suffer from these differences.

My first impression of protective services social work was that of renewed culture shock. The abuses that I had read about in adoption files were now there for me to see firsthand. I could well understand how workers might burn out quickly. My second impression was how important it was to have a cohesive group of people to work with, and how important it was to order one's own private life so that there was maximum support when the cases got to you and you were feeling especially low. It made me think of something I had heard about severe storms like hurricanes. There always seems to be an eye, a center where things are absolutely calm, while on the outside the storm rages its fury. How necessary it is to be at that center personally, to experience the calm, when the world of your work is in constant turmoil.

I was glad that my unit seemed to be a congenial group of people. Our supervisor, Mike, was a joker who often made light of situations. At first, I found his manner disturbing, but once I got into the work, I also realized that it was necessary for him. He had started as a worker and had been with the agency for quite a few years. Those who did not leave after a short time often made a career out of it. He was considerably older than I was and had three children who were nearing their teens. He used to joke about how life with three soon-to-be-teenagers wouldn't be much different from coming to the office. Tony, one of my coworkers, was a large man who had probably excelled at football in his school days. He joked that maybe we would be investigating Mike for abuse once his children were fully into their teen years. Tony's somewhat younger children were also a handful, and I wondered how parents managed to keep their home lives and their work separate.

Donna and Rosemary completed our unit. Both had been with the unit for a little over a year. Donna was in her 30's and unmarried, while Rosemary had a teenage son. She was a chain smoker and did her part to fog up the office. In those days, there were no prohibitions against smoking, and due to the stress of the job, there were many smokers who spent their day in the office puffing and coughing. In fact, I was the only one in the unit who did not smoke, and I found the infrequent unit meetings that actually got held to be foggy affairs in Mike's smoke-filled office. I could not wait to get out of there!

Now public office buildings are smoke free, a fact that gives rise to the numerous workers who stand outside the front door, regardless of the temperature, to have their smoke break. My smoker friends tell me that it is a great inconvenience, but I enjoy the cleaner air in the office. Each to his or her own, I guess.

By the end of the first day, there were six folders piled on my desk. Training, I learned, was on the job. It was like being thrown into a deep pool of water and learning to swim for survival. I am envious of the new workers today who are usually given some training, often for a full week. I did have an opportunity to shadow other workers once again, but since I had transferred from another office, it was expected that I would know a bit about the job. I did feel fairly comfortable with the foster home visits. Those were familiar. But working with the birth parents would be new for me.

The first case on my desk would actually become one of my most frustrating and finally my favorite. Gina and Rudy became one of my success stories although some people might question how I measure success. Gina was a thirty-year-old woman who had three daughters, ages seven, nine, and twelve. She was also pregnant when I first met her. Gina was a frustrated artist who had never had an opportunity to develop her talent, and satisfied herself by drawing on napkins, on the back of bills, or whatever was available to her. For years, I had several of Gina's beautiful drawings. I finally took her a drawing pad and one would have thought that I had given her the best gift ever. She had been married to a man who, I was convinced, had populated the entire city as I would encounter numerous children who bore his name. When Gina discovered yet one more infidelity, she left him, taking their three daughters with her. For a time she received welfare, but was ashamed to continue, so she worked three jobs to make ends meet. When she contracted breast cancer, a friend convinced her to place her children while she recovered. Reluctantly, she did, but took them back before she had even finished her treatments.

"I missed them so much," she had told me when we talked about her past.

Then Gina had met Rudy, a fifty-eight-year-old man who had been married four times. His matrimonial failures did not seem to be due to any irresponsibility on his part, but rather because he had a knack for choosing women who "did him wrong." His first wife put him in serious debt while she slept around and treated her lovers with Rudy's money. Wife number two stole a large amount of money he was carrying to the bank for his boss, getting him fired and put on trial for embezzlement until she was uncovered as the real culprit. His third wife moved her entire family into the apartment, and made Rudy support them while he was made to sleep on the couch. And wife number four was a lesbian who wanted children and needed a donor. Of course, she did not tell Rudy this until after she and her female lover, who lived with the couple, had the two children they wanted. Then they left, taking both children and all the furniture. The fact that they then neglected and sexually abused the children brought children's protective services into their lives and into Rudy's. It was not surprising that when Rudy met gentle, honest Gina, he would believe that he had died and gone to heaven. They set up house, and Rudy asked to have his children from wife number four returned to him.

Why Gina would take on hard-luck Rudy and his two daughters, one of whom was mentally retarded, was a mystery to all, but the two were devoted to one another. The case had been assigned to me to supervise their care of Betty Jane and Mercy Ann, Rudy's daughters who were in the couple's care. The fact that wife number four had asked to have the children returned to her created a battle of no small proportions. Over the next four years, I would make regular visits to Gina to give her support as she attempted to care for five children and the two more she would have with Rudy, and fend off the various acts of vandalism and attempts at suit that wife number four would level against the struggling couple. But I would come to admire Gina's simple honesty and perseverance, and she, I believe, began to look at me as a mentor. It was not the typical relationship between social worker and client, but it was a rewarding one for both of us.

My second case on that first day in protective services involved a twenty-four-year-old prostitute, one of whose two children had just died from neglect. While Mava Melanson plied her trade with successful businessmen and reported to her well-supported "manager," her two children were seriously neglected. Five-month-old Tyrone had died from this neglect, and eighteen-month-old Lissy (for Melissa) was so lethargic that she neither sat up nor crawled, much less walked. A petition had been filed, attesting to the mother's inability to care for her daughter, while a criminal complaint was pending giving her the responsibility for Tyrone's death. The hearing would soon be held, and it was up to me to support the allegations of Mom's neglect.

"Juvenile court hearings are a piece of cake," Mike told me in his usual offhanded manner. "Don't sweat it! You'll be in and out in no time." The cigarette held in his mouth bounced as he spoke, and his eyes, as usual, were half closed to shield them from the smoke.

Two other cases stood out for me as I read over my new files. Irene Harper was the mother of five children, all of whom had been removed from her because she was unable to control her substance abuse and frequently left them alone. Terri was the oldest at fifteen. Her younger brothers, thirteen-year-old Howie, ten-year-old Eddie, nine-year-old Paul, and eight-year-old Mickey had all had some form of problem in their foster homes. They were described as difficult, and Howie had even come before juvenile court for stealing a car. He was currently on probation. The baby, Ellen, was only three. The worker before me had worked hard with this Mom and had finally returned Terri and the baby to her when she seemed to be doing well. Our job was to supervise for the next year to determine if Irene was able to keep her sobriety and care for her two children. If that was the case, the boys might be returned to her.

"Terri is a sweetheart, her last worker said," Mike filled me in on what he knew of the case. "I guess she was holding things together when the kids were removed last time. It's important to make sure that she doesn't get stuck doing that again."

Two of the cases were assessments that had to be completed before the children were referred to the adoption unit. Those would be easy enough, I thought. I certainly knew what an adoption worker would want to know.

The final case would be a bit challenging, Mike told me.

"Dawn Whitedeer has had two children taken from her already, because of neglect. She is American Indian and moved here from out west. Where she came from, kids were allowed to wander freely. But there's a small problem here: she lives in one of the roughest parts of the city, and when a three-year-old is found wandering around after dark, there's a problem. In this case, the child was picked up by a notorious pedophile that loves very young girls. The police picked him up on a speeding violation and figured out that the kid wasn't his," Mike puffed, and a cloud of smoke surrounded his head.

"Was the baby hurt?" I asked, expecting the worst.

"The police wanted her checked over. What's her name?" he flipped through the record in search of information. "Here it is, Star Whitedeer. It did not appear that she had been penetrated. They guess that he had just found her and was speeding to get to somewhere to stash her while he sexually abused her."

My stomach felt queasy. A three-year-old! I thought of how Reg Forrester had greeted me. Was this really the real world? Ugh!

"Anyway, there was a petition filed in juvenile court saying that Dawn had failed to protect her child. Star is now in foster care, and we are trying to work with Ms. Whitedeer to help her recognize some of the finer points of becoming parent of the year in the inner city," Mike's sarcasm was something I would soon get used to. Along with his sometimes misplaced humor, it apparently armed him to face the job. "But it ain't easy. This one just ain't buying this parenting stuff!" he finished with an ironic smile.

"So that's your team," Mike closed the last file and lit up again. "Have a nice ballgame, little lady!"

I decided that I missed Herb's supervisory style, and felt lucky to have had him as my first supervisor.

As I thought of how I would schedule my visits, I started getting confused. Now, was Betty Jane a Harper or Gina's daughter? Which baby died? Okay, that's it, I thought, time to make my lists again.

I sat down with the small black notebook that would become my friend and protector for the next few years, and began to summarize my cases, each case on a separate page.

Page #1- Solander/Kaplan

Gina Solander (30 years old, Caucasian) & Rudy Kaplan (58 years old, Caucasian)

Shawna – age 12

Sherryl – age 9

Crystal – age 7

Betty Jane – age 7

Mercy Ann – age 6 (mentally retarded)

Gina pregnant with Rudy's child and due in a month. BJ and MA removed from their mother and placed with Rudy. Mother and her lesbian partner have visits with the girls.

Page #2- Harper

Irene Harper (37 years old Caucasian, divorced, history of alcoholism. Married three times.)

Terri – age 15 (from Mom's 1st marriage)

Howie – age 13 (1st marriage. On probation for being involved in stealing a car.)

Eddie – age 10 (2nd marriage)

Paul – age 9 (2nd marriage)

Ellen – age 3 (Born out of wedlock after second husband left and before third)

Terri and Ellen recently returned to Mom. Supervise Mom. If doing well, arrange to return boys. Boys may also need evaluations due to behavior problems.

Page # 3 – Melanson

Mava Melanson (26 years old, Black, never married, prostitute)

Melissa (Lissy) – age 18 months (severely delayed development)

Tyrone – died of neglect at 5 months

Juvenile court hearing (neglect) scheduled. Criminal court hearing (criminal neglect resulting in death) also pending. Lissy placed in foster home until hearing.

Page # 4 – Whitedeer

> Dawn Whitedeer (22 years old, Native American, marriage status unknown)
>
> Star – age 3, abducted and possibly sexually abused by pedophile
>
> Work with mother on parenting skills and possible return of Star. Child placed in a foster home. Schedule a psychological evaluation of child to determine effects of abduction.

On the last two pages, I listed information about the two routine adoption assessments. Well, I thought, surveying what I had written. I certainly had my work cut out for me!

Questions for Thought

1. Have you considered graduate school? If you are in graduate school, what made you first consider it? What would motivate one to go to graduate school?

2. At what point do we know that it is time to move on to a new challenge?

3. Is it okay to date a former supervisor? Why or why not? Would you ever date someone who currently supervised you? Why or why not?

4. What was your initial impression of Gina and Rudy? How do you think it would be to work with them?

5. What are your feelings about Mava Melanson? How might that influence your working with her?

6. How would you feel about working with Irene Harper or Dawn Whitedeer? Which of all these cases might be the most challenging for you? Why?

17

A Different World

I took Mike's offer to have me shadow several workers to determine how to approach clients who knew that, at any moment, you could take their children from their lives forever. Content that I understood the approach, even though I was not always comfortable with it, I proceeded to make appointments for my own cases. Gina Solander's seemed like the most worker friendly situation, so I decided to start with her.

It is strange the way cities take on geographic personalities. Cases, especially those involving neglect, seem to cluster themselves in certain neighborhoods. During my years in Protective Services, my clients tended to be in three distinct areas, and I found myself working in these places unless I was visiting a foster home or seeing cases in the smaller towns. I found it interesting that Gina's triple-decker home was situated on the edge of one of these sections. Dark gray like many in the neighborhood, there had been some obvious attempts to fix up this building while those near it stood as a testament to the neglect of their owners. The stairs to the second floor, where Gina and her brood made their home, were relatively clean, and I was glad that for my first call at least, I did not have to dodge the critters that Mike had warned me about.

An affectionate calico cat rubbed against my legs as I rang the bell. I thought quickly about what I had read of Gina. She had been born of middle class parents who apparently could not accept the myriad of problems that plagued the middle of their three daughters. They had her club foot repaired, and sought treatment for her thyroid problems and severe eczema, but Gina had never fit in. When she married a man twice her age who was known for his unsavory reputation, her parents decided that Gina had not repaid them for their care, and now had nothing to do with her. Somehow, Gina had found the strength to be a survivor. She survived her parents disowning her, her husband's beating and infidelities, and took her children and left him. After her divorce, she had successfully survived cancer and now was, by all reports, doing well as the caretaker for her own and Rudy's children. I was not sure what I expected when a sandy-haired woman, looking plain and ordinary in her faded maternity smock, opened the door to me. But the smile that brightened her face when I introduced myself transformed the ordinary into a lovely visage of warmth and caring. I would learn many lessons from this young woman, not the least of which concerned the strength of the human spirit.

"I was so glad to get your call," she told me. "They told me that I would have a new worker soon."

Gina ushered me into an old kitchen that might have looked shabby had it not been for its cleanliness and attempt at little decorative touches. The calico cat scooted in with me and purred at her feet. Patting the cat briefly, she led me to the table adorned by a vase of dried flowers. She moved with a limp and the heaviness of late pregnancy, but rather than making her ungainly, she seemed to travel in a rolling motion that was not unbecoming.

"I just put on coffee and I baked some muffins. Would you like some?"

What is so bad about this work, I thought, as I bit into an apple muffin and sipped steaming coffee.

"I am so worried about Betty Jane," she began, after we had our coffee and had had a chance for small talk. During that time I learned that, as I had expected, the children were at school and Rudy at work. "She has visits with her mother, but when she comes home from Trudy's, her mom's, her behavior is awful. She wets herself for days afterward, and I had her trained. And last night I caught her trying to stick a hairbrush," she stopped, looking embarrassed, but apparently decided that the story must be told. "She was trying to put a hairbrush up her private parts."

Gina took a sip of her coffee, as if for courage, and went on.

"I think that Trudy's abusing her again. She used to, you know. That's why the State people," she hesitated, with a quick look at me as if to say "Sorry, do you mind being called that?" When I did not seem to object or respond, she continued, "They took the girls away, because of the abuse and because she wasn't taking care of them. You should have seen them. Poor little kids!"

Gina jumped, laughing, and put a hand on her bulging stomach.

"He sure is itching to be born!" she said, with a smile of anticipation on her thin face.

"Do you know it's a boy?" I asked, hoping to gain a few minutes to think about the situation with Betty Jane's mother.

"Not by any tests or anything. But I just know it is," Gina responded confidently.

"More?" she asked, pointing to my coffee cup. When I declined, she started to take away the cup, but seemed to have a thought in the middle of the act. She paused, saying, "Do you think the judge could do anything? Like maybe we have to be there when she sees the girls or something?" As she spoke, I noticed her long, graceful fingers with their tapered nails. The thought occurred to me that she could have played the piano. I remembered my mother saying that long fingers are ideal for piano playing. Then suddenly I realized that she had just hit upon a possible solution for the problems with Trudy and her daughter.

"That's a good idea," I agreed. "Let me ask if we can have visiting changed to supervised visits. We might also have Betty Jane evaluated. It does sound like something is happening on the visits." To myself, I considered asking that the visits be stopped altogether. If the mother was abusing Betty Jane, it hardly seemed like the best place for the child to visit.

Gina seemed content that I heard her concerns, and was willing to look into it.

"She doesn't visit again for two weeks. Will you know by then?" I assured her that I would check into it and give her a call. Gina was thoughtful for a moment. She picked up a pen and idly doodled in her napkin.

"She never even wants to see Mercy Ann. Trudy, I mean. It makes me sad. Mercy can't help it if she doesn't think like other people. When Trudy calls to arrange the visit, she always has some excuse for Mercy not coming. Then she cries and cries. Poor little Mercy Ann. I feel so bad for her."

Parental visits can be so difficult for children, especially if one child is favored over another. I could imagine how the mentally retarded girl was hurt by her mother's rejection. A look of pain crossed Gina's face and she grabbed her abdomen again. She closed her eyes and inhaled deeply, seeming to ride out the feeling.

"Oh no," she breathed, as the pain apparently subsided. "I'm not ready for you, baby! You have another three weeks!"

"Have any of the others been early?" I asked, wondering if I would add mid-wifery to my duties. But she was relaxed now, and smiled her easy smile.

"No, and I don't expect this one will be either," She looked down, and I did too. I was amazed to see that the napkin had been transformed into the image of a fairy creature.

"That's lovely!" I exclaimed.

"Oh, it's nothing," she said dismissively, crumpling the napkin.

"Oh but it is!" I took the napkin from her and smoothed it out on the table. Gina looked embarrassed.

"I just love fairies," she explained, as if in defense. "My grandmother used to read me stories about little woodland creatures, and I fell in love with the idea. It makes life a bit more beautiful. You can have that if you want," she finished self consciously, as if she was sure that I would discard it as she was going to.

"I'd like that. Thank you," It was the first of my Gina drawings, and a window into the incredible capabilities of this remarkable young woman.

We talked a bit more about her children and about her plans to fix up the baby's room. The apartment was large, and Gina told me that there were four small bedrooms.

"Right now, Shawna and Sherryl are in one and the little girls in another. We'll have to do some juggling when the baby comes. He'll be in our room for a few months, and then who knows. Shawna wants her own room, so we'll see." I thought of the spacious house that I had grown up in, and did not envy Gina with six children in one apartment.

Suddenly, the floor seemed to erupt with a flurry of angry words and crashes. The words were inaudible, but the sentiments were obvious. Gina cringed, and I wondered if she was seeing echoes of her own past as an abused wife. There was another loud crash, and a door being slammed, and then it was quiet.

"That's the only problem with this place," she said, in a quiet voice. "The people downstairs are always fighting. Rudy tried to butt in once. It was summer, and all the windows were open and the kids were scared. The guy was out in the yard, and he was punching the woman and screaming all these dirty words at her. So Rudy tried to stop it. The guy beat him up real good. We had to go to the hospital. He broke Rudy's rib. Since then, we don't dare do anything. And they have been out to get us ever since. They killed a cat we had," she looked at the calico curled up on a nearby chair. "I tried to keep Patches in, but she gets out. Now, we just let her go and hope she will be okay. And they've put sugar in Rudy's gas tank. That wrecked the engine. We are really afraid of them. We told the landlord, he doesn't live in the building, and he said he couldn't do anything. They're his wife's cousins, and he has to let them stay."

A look of pain crossed her face again. She looked concerned after the pain had subsided.

"Is there anyone you can call to take you to the hospital if this is labor?" I asked, hoping that she knew someone more experienced than I was.

"Rudy will come home if he has to," she told me. "Or I can take a taxi."

"A taxi?" my incredulousness must have showed how naïve I still was. I could not imagine having no support system in a time like this.

"Sure," she said, unconcerned. "I did for two of my others. I can go down to the clinic if I am concerned. There'll be someone on duty there." In later years, when my concerned husband would speed me to the hospital as I anticipated the presence of my own obstetricians to whom I had become so attached, convinced they were vital to my children's trouble-free births, I thought of Gina. Alone but for hard working Rudy, and dependent upon whatever doctor was on duty at the clinic, Gina had had three, and then four children, without the care that I had come to expect.

After assuring me that she would be fine, Gina ushered me out her door. As I descended the stairs, I had to avoid a broken wooden chair that lay at the door of the apartment below. I wondered whose head it had been broken over, and was thankful that I had not had to leave half an hour earlier.

Not far from Gina's home was that of Dawn Whitedeer, so I decided that this was as good a time as any to talk with her about the return of her three-year-old daughter, Star. The Whitedeer home, also a triple-decker, had little resemblance to Gina's. Painted at one time a dull green, it was peeling and weather-beaten. The front stairs looked like one was taking a chance climbing them, not only because of their condition, but because of the two scruffy women sitting at the top, clad in faded housedresses. One had a broom propped nearby. The woman showed no inclination toward cleaning, however, and sat with a cloud of cigarette smoke above her head that was so thick it was difficult to discern her features. The other puffed on a corn-cob pipe, something that amazed me in the heart of a northern city.

"Who ya want?" barked the broom-lady through the smoke, apparently assessing my hesitant survey of the house.

"Whitedeer?"

As the smoked cleared slightly, the old woman cackled, displaying gums that should have held a set of teeth.

"Round back. Third floor," she said, gesturing with an emaciated arm. I moved gingerly around several unidentified blobs of brown on the ground and made my way toward the back of the house.

"She probably ain't home!" came the call in my wake.

A long outside stairway led to the third floor. I calculated my chances of successfully ascending it without crashing through to the ground. The odds didn't appear that great, but I decided that I had no choice. Although the stairs creaked threateningly, they bore my weight, and I was soon at a dirty doorway far above the yard below. Several loud knocks were rewarded by an opening door. A very large woman with long, greasy black hair and deep brown, albeit clouded eyes, greeted me silently. She was dressed in a long, flowing muumuu that was well overdue for a wash. She smelled of body odor mingled with an acrid, weedy smell that I recognized, from my college fascination with American Indian lore, as sweet grass. I introduced myself, and she hesitated, as if trying to decide how not to have this visit. Apparently deciding that she could not avoid it, she turned and went back into the room, leaving the door open. I assumed that this was her idea of an invitation, and followed her in. The kitchen was large and cluttered. On the kitchen table was a wooden bowl that smoked with what I assumed was the sweet grass. Surrounding it were a collection of beer bottles, ashtrays brimming with cigarette butts, and the remnants of several days' worth of half-consumed TV dinners. I suspected that without the burning sweet grass, the odor might have been worse than it was. I also found the combination incongruous, as sweet grass is often burned to help an individual center. The other items spoke more of addiction and escape.

The floor was cluttered with a variety of substances that I was not sure I was eager to know the origin of. Dawn lowered her bulk onto a kitchen chair and lit up another cigarette. Had I not been there, her affect would have been no different. I looked around quickly, remembering the admonition of my coworkers not to sit on any stuffed furniture that could also be the home of a myriad of six-legged creatures. The other kitchen chair seemed fairly safe, and I sat down. The kitchen was ringed by three doors, most of which were partially open, but not enough for me to see inside. A very mangy cat emerged from one door, and I prayed that he would not rub against my leg. But he seemed as disinterested in me as his owner, and drifted into another room without paying us any heed.

In my best social work manner, I explained to Dawn Whitedeer that we were interested in returning Star to her, if that was what she would like. To do so, we must insure that she was able to prevent what had happened to her daughter, being unsupervised and kidnapped by a pedophile, from happening again. It became obvious that she was not impressed by my best social work tones. In fact, she made no response. She sat, puffing on her cigarette and looking off into space. The sweet grass burned silently, making the air feel close and stifling.

I was composing my thoughts for another try when Dawn Whitedeer got up and ambled to the door of one of the rooms, passed through it, and closed it firmly. Okay, I thought, an urgent bathroom call. Waiting, I looked around. The cat emerged from a half open door and pushed it open a bit more. Aha! The bathroom. If that was the bathroom, where was Dawn? I am not sure how long it took me to get the message that Ms. Whitedeer had no intention of continuing our one-sided conversation. When I finally came to that realization, feeling very stupid, I called out "Ms. Whitedeer?" It shouldn't have surprised me that there was no answer from behind the closed door.

Another attempt at calling and I decided that I looked like a real idiot. I ripped a piece of paper from my notebook and scribbled a note saying that I would call her. I called more loudly that I was leaving and that there was a note on the table. I imagined Dawn Whitedeer breathing a sigh of relief on the other side of the door.

Once outside I noticed that the women had disappeared. I hoped, but doubted from the look of them, that it was to make use of the broom. I breathed deeply, expelling the odor of sweet grass from my lungs. Forever after, the smell of burning weeds would bring to mind that day when I stood outside of Dawn Whitedeer's door.

Mava Melanson did not answer when I knocked on her door. It too was on the edge of the neighborhood, but appeared cleaner than the one I had just left. I could not imagine that she would be plying her trade in the middle of the day. More likely, she was sleeping. Unable to wake her, I started to leave. A long, black Lincoln was parked in my path as I started to cross the street to my car. With a mechanical buzz, the passenger's side window rolled slowly down and a large Black man with a shaved head and an earring on one ear regarded me suspiciously. Even in that brief moment, I could see that he was bedecked in gold chains and sported a fashionable shirt. I wondered if this was Mava's infamous pimp, but decided that I really didn't want to ask. I moved around the car, willing him not to stop me. He opened the driver's window and continued to stare at me. Message received, I decided, and concluded that I would wait until the court hearing to make the acquaintance of Ms. Melanson.

Well, one out of two, I thought, considering my two unsuccessful contacts. I decided that a foster home might be more rewarding, but a call to Star's foster home was met with a ringing phone and no answer.

Back at the office, I was met by a harried Mike.

"Oh, I'm glad you're here," he told me. "Rosemary is in court, and one of her cases just got called in. Could you go out on it?" He filled me in on the case, assuming that I had agreed. It was a five-year-old boy who was an open case of my colleague, Rosemary. He had been severely abused by Mom's boyfriend when the case originally came in. Rosemary had been working with her, and although Mom was not willing to give up the boyfriend, there had been no more beatings of Toby. Now a neighbor called in saying that she had heard screams in the early hours of the morning, and suspected that Toby was again being beaten. We wondered why it had taken her so long to call, as it was already early afternoon. But Mike felt that, in Rosemary's absence, someone should go out.

"I was going out on it," he told me between puffs. "But lucky you can take it since you are here." Lucky me, gee thanks, I thought.

The Ambertino apartment was situated in a housing project on the outskirts of the city. Built within the last five years, the dwellings still maintained some semblance of attractiveness to their cheaply constructed units. I imagined that in a few years, this project would be as run-down as the one I had seen on the other side of the city. At least this one did not have the reputation for being as unsafe for social workers as the other project had. Each unit had four apartments contained within it, and a high fence circling the outside to form a back and side yard. I could hear children playing behind the fence of number 152.

Jewel Ambertino was deeply involved in her soap operas when I knocked at her door. She fished in the pocket of her shirt, drew out a cigarette, and lit it. Did she intentionally blow smoke in my face, or was it my imagination? Her black hair hung to her shoulders, and she flipped it back in agitation. The television blared in the background, and illuminated the room that was darkened by the pulled shades.

"Yeah?" she stood with one hand on her hip, letting me know that there were other things she would rather be doing than greeting me. I introduced myself, and before I could explain more about the reason for my visit, she interrupted.

"I got a social worker! She was just out last week!"

"We have had a report that Toby may have been injured. Mrs. Caruski is in court, and I am here to see Toby." I felt like the ultimate bad guy when I saw Mrs. Ambertino's look of terror. Then her face cleared, and she inhaled on her cigarette again. Another exhale in my direction.

"Okay," she said, seemingly resigned. "Come in. I'll get Toby." She left me alone with the loud sobs of some girl who had just discovered that her best friend was pregnant by her husband who had just beat her up and then promised to take her to Bermuda. Who needed soap operas, I thought. I had my work.

Mrs. Ambertino reappeared with an adorable blonde boy whose huge blue eyes stared at me in what appeared to be mistrust.

"Here's Toby," said the mother, thrusting him toward me. She returned to her program, leaving me with the child. But it was clear that she was watching us carefully out of the corner of her eye.

The child's fair complexion looked unblemished. He had certainly not been beaten. I asked his permission, getting a nod of approval, and lifted his shirt. No bruises anywhere. Toby was silent. I asked after my examination if anyone had hit him, and he shook his blonde curls.

"See, I tol' ya!" snapped Jewel. "It was probably that old woman in apartment 160." She continued to describe her neighbor and her nosiness with a string of expletives that were far from complimentary. I agreed that there must have been a mistake, and left her to find out if her heroine would get to Bermuda.

It was past 2:00 and I realized that I was hungry as I drove back to the office. I might as well grab a hamburger to go and read some of the new cases that I knew Mike had for me. I was anxious to get home early, as I had promised Herb that I would fix him a special dinner tonight. He had gotten the promotion at the adoption unit, and although we planned to go out over the weekend, I thought I'd like to fix him something special for an early celebration.

With hamburger in hand and a drink from the machine, I sat down to read when Rosemary came over to my desk.

"How was court?"

"Ugh!" she responded. "The turkey of a judge just went to a seminar on parents' rights. So the kids have to endure another return to the parents until the Mom beats them up again. Great, huh?" But she quickly remembered what was on her mind.

"Mike said that someone called on Ambertino. What's the story?" I told her about my visit and my failure to find any marks on Toby.

"That's been an awful case," Rosemary confided. "Mom will not get rid of that useless boyfriend. She's got a couple of girls too, but that boyfriend takes it out on poor Toby. He and Mom have a really combative relationship. I figure he takes it out on Toby 'cause he looks like Mom, but he doesn't have the guts to beat her up. He tried once, and she split his head open with a beer bottle. Toby's a good substitute, I guess."

Suddenly, something that Rosemary said hit me.

"Looks like Mom? What do you mean?"

Rosemary eyed me questioningly. "You know, same coloring, same eyes. Why?"

I thought of the blonde haired, blue eyed child I had seen at Ambertinos'. As I told Rosemary, her expression became grim.

"That sounds like she showed you Matthew Morgan. He lives next door. We had that case, but Mom is doing okay now. We have to get to the bottom of this one. Can you go back out there with me?" she asked. I glanced at my watch and realized that there might not be a special dinner for Herb tonight.

"Sure, let's go."

Mrs. Ambertino's expression when she saw the two of us on her doorstep suggested that she should never play poker, despite her bluff earlier. Taken by surprise, her children were now inside, and Rosemary spotted Toby immediately. His left eye was almost shut and there was a deep gash over it. A piece of one ear was missing, and his arms and legs were both badly bruised. Rosemary, who apparently knew the child well, got down on her knees beside him and observed his wounds. Tears began to stream down his face as he watched his social worker.

"Who did this to you, honey?" she asked softly, in a voice trained by years of motherhood and equally as many as a social worker with children. "Was it Henry?"

The child nodded silently and winced at the effort.

"We need to have a doctor look at these, honey. Don't be afraid. I'll stay with you. We can't let Henry do this to you again."

Rosemary stood up and looked at the now weeping mother. "I explained what would happen, Jewel, if you let him at Toby again. We are going to take him to the emergency room. I will call you from there." She gently ushered Toby to the waiting car as Mrs. Ambertino followed us screaming "You can't take him! You can't take my baby!"

Rosemary got him into the car and I sat beside him as she dealt with the weeping mother. "Your baby has been beaten once too often by your boyfriend," I heard her say, and then tried to distract Toby, lest he hear more of the interchange.

"Henry!" Mrs. Ambertino's scream resonated through the closed windows. A wiry man was barreling toward us, both fists clenched in obvious anger. I felt Toby shrink to half his size in the seat beside me.

"It's okay," I soothed, as much for myself as for the child. We both watched as the drama unfolded around us. With a whack in Jewel's direction, Henry addressed himself in an angry charade to Rosemary. Social workers learn that, despite their harsh words, most child abusers will not strike out at an adult. In fact, it is their fear of other adults that causes them to take out their abuse on the smaller members of the household. But I also knew that there were exceptions, and Henry looked enraged enough to be the exception. I silently calculated when or if I should get out of the car and back up Rosemary. I had little confidence in my brawn, but I thought that if Henry knew there were two of us, it might help. On the other hand, Rosemary was renowned in the office for her ability to handle tough situations, and I was rooting for her. I did not want to take the chance of leaving a bruised and frightened child to either bolt in fear or be ripped from the car by an angry Henry. Before my mental dialogue came to a satisfactory conclusion, Henry had quieted and Rosemary seemed to be getting the upper hand. A moment later, she slid into the car, slammed the door, and sped off with a deep exhalation of breath, "Let's get out of here!"

We left Henry and a weeping Jewel in our dust. I hoped that he would not turn his wrath on her.

"What did you say?" I wondered at Rosemary's calming of the storm. I looked at Toby, who nestled against me.

"I reminded him that I knew that there was a warrant out on him and he had better watch it or I'd get the police." She told me, now able to smile.

"Lucky you knew that!" I said.

"I didn't," Rosemary confessed. "Just a lucky guess!" I began to understand where her fame had originated.

We had Toby's wounds checked out. While we waited, Rosemary said, "Thanks for being here today. Couldn't have done it without you!"

"You're kidding, right?" I asked incredulously.

"Nope, teamwork's what it's all about. Come on, I'll take you to your car. I have to take Toby to a foster home tonight and that won't be tough."

I agreed, realizing that I was exhausted. There would obviously be no celebration dinner for Herb tonight. Maybe I'd stop on the way home and pick up Chinese food.

Questions for Thought _____

1. How would you feel, knowing that you had the power to take children from their parents? How would these feelings temper your actions?

2. What strengths do you see in Gina? What are her problems?

3. What was your impression of Dawn Whitedeer? How might you have handled the visit?

4. How would you have felt when watched by the man in the car outside the Melanson apartment? How might you have handled the situation?

5. How would you have felt after talking to Rosemary about the Ambertino case? How might you have handled the interview?

6. How would you have handled Henry?

18

Fickle Lady Justice

The halls of the juvenile court were lined with people. Social workers paced, nervously awaiting delayed clients. Lawyers whispered in corners to youths and their parents, some of whom looked frightened. For others, the experience was one that had been oft-repeated, and their boredom was obvious. This was my first day in juvenile court, and I would admit that I was nervous. Mike had sent Tony, another one of my colleagues along, as he knew the ropes in court.

"It's a piece of cake," remarked Tony as we joined the throng waiting to be called. "That's her, by the way," Tony said under his breath as we passed an elegant and overdressed Black woman in high heels. Beside her was a tall, medium-complected man whose stance said that he felt and looked incredibly confident.

"Her pimp?" I whispered to Tony, who laughed aloud.

"Her lawyer," he shot back.

We leaned against a far wall where we could watch Mava Melanson. I had no doubt that she was successful at her trade. She was an elegant creature with perfectly rounded curves, high breasts, and gorgeous, shapely legs. Her clothes looked expensive, and her demeanor made her stand out from the other clients in the room.

"The lawyer's from Hartwell, Black, and Chapin. Bill Chapin," Tony told me, and at a questioning look he continued, "It's one of the better law firms in the city. These gals can afford it."

"These gals?"

"Yeah, Ms. Melanson is one of Jerome Tyre's stable. He is a big-time manager from Providence. We're not playing with small change here. This is serious prostitution. This lady doesn't have any small-bit customers. Only the guys with big bucks use her," Tony explained.

"Why would anyone like that have children?" I asked, hardly believing the world I had walked into.

"Who knows," Tony chewed on a toothpick as I had often seen him do. He said that it helped him not to smoke more than he already did, which, in my book, was too much. But the court did not allow smoking in its corridors, so I understood Tony's need for the toothpick. "Sometimes they slip up on the old birth control, and maybe some of them just get that motherly feeling."

"She hardly looks like the motherly type," I mused, watching the beautifully coifed woman as she conversed with her attorney.

"Does our side get an attorney?" I asked after a bit.

"Oh sure, there's an attorney for the kids. Red Mitchell, but he usually manages to blow in about court time. Don't know how he does it. The rest of us wait around for hours and old Red makes it right on time. We keep thinking that someday he'll miss a hearing, but he never does. He's not a bad attorney and is usually appointed by the court to represent the children. But he may have met his match in Chapin."

It was a good hour before our case was called. By that time, Tony had demolished six toothpicks, and I expected him to spit out slivers. His shirt was sticking to his large frame, and I realized that it had gotten a bit hot with all the bodies pressed in one small area. Mava Melanson continued to look cool and confident, and I envied her composure under the circumstances. How could a woman look like this when one of her children had died as a result of her neglect and the other had been taken from her? Predictably, Red Mitchell made his appearance just before we were called, and I was quickly introduced to him.

"Welcome to the world of insanity," he said, pumping my hand vigorously. "The only sideshow in town with such potential for dire consequences."

I looked at Tony with a "who is this guy" look, but my colleague just laughed and shrugged.

When our case was called, Mava and her attorney preceded us into the courtroom. Juvenile court is hardly what one expects. More like a classroom than a courtroom, the judge's bench isn't even raised in many courts. In this courtroom it was raised slightly, but nothing like the criminal or probate courts I had seen. Two long tables sat at the front of the room, with only a row or two of seats behind them.

"Juvenile court is a closed courtroom," Tony explained. "Only the client, the attorneys, probation, the clerk, and the assigned social workers are allowed. I had to practically get a papal dispensation to come with you. On the first hearing, the child appears briefly, to be identified. That was a couple of weeks ago. This hearing is to review the facts and to determine custody of the child until an investigation can take place. It'll be over in a minute. You'll see."

If I had any illusions of being out in a minute, I was sadly mistaken. Attorney Chapin earned his money as he shot questions at me about the procedures used by our Department when the children had been taken. Fortunately, I knew the file, but was still forced to remind the judge on several occasions that I had just picked up the case. Testifying for almost an hour, I glanced at Tony for support. He shrugged and looked sheepish, and I wished that I was anywhere but there. After reviewing the facts in great detail, the attorney suggested that it was the incompetence of the Department that had caused baby Tyrone's death, rather than parental neglect. I found it hard to believe that facts such as these could be so skewed.

After several hours, the judge looked sternly at both our table and Mava Melanson's and proclaimed that since the case was also being heard in criminal court on a criminal neglect complaint, he would not make a ruling until that case was settled. In the meantime, Melissa Melanson, age eighteen months, would remain in the custody of the Department and reside in foster care.

"I don't believe it!" I fumed when Tony and I had bid goodbye to Red Mitchell and were returning to the car. "All that time and for what?"

"Welcome to the world of court," said my colleague, unlocking the doors of his Jeep. "It is rare that a case of neglect is heard in both juvenile and criminal court, but it happens all the time with sexual abuse. Judges don't want to step on each other's toes."

"But it seems so clear that she doesn't want that child. How can she? And she did kill another one."

"Nothing's clear-cut," mused Tony. "I've seen cases that you are sure you won't lose go down the tubes because of some technicality or due to a smart attorney. Lady Justice, she is fickle," he mimicked in an amusing voice, balancing his book on one hand and mine on the other.

"What about the best interests of the child? I remembered our discussion of this in graduate school. Child welfare should be based on what is in the child's best interests."

"Everyone has rights," Tony said sarcastically. "Even hookers and junkies!"

Tony dropped me at the office, where I picked up my own car. Frustrated, but unable to get the case out of my mind, I decided to visit Mava's child in the foster home. I had yet to visit her, though I had talked to the foster mother on the phone. I gave her a quick call from the office and she said that she would be glad to see me. She had known that the case was going to court, and had hoped I would call and tell her what happened.

Melissa Melanson (who the foster mother said was called Lissy) was the only foster child of Tammy Howard and her husband, Biff. Tammy was a vivacious mother of her own three children. I liked her immediately. Lissy was their first foster child, and had been quite a culture shock for the expectant family.

"You wouldn't have believed her when she came," Tammy told me when we had gotten the introductions and formalities out of the way. We sat in the family's small living room sipping soda that Tammy had provided. Lissy sat in a baby seat munching on a cracker. It was difficult to imagine that this obese and unattractive child could possibly be the offspring of the elegant creature I had seen earlier in court. Lissy was much lighter than her dark-skinned mother, suggesting that her father was probably Caucasian. Her fat face rarely smiled, and she had minimum control over her large body.

"She was so dirty!" Tammy went on. "She had lice and smelled so bad. They said that her brother died and she's so fat because she lived on Kool Aid. She was just a blob. She's actually learned to sit up since she came, and the doctor says that once we get her weight down, she'll probably be able to crawl and then walk. My kids were all running by her age." Tammy watched the baby with what was obviously growing affection. I wondered if Tammy had any idea of how different her children's childhoods must have been from that of Lissy. As if picking up on my thoughts, she commented, "Is it true that her Mom is a prostitute?" She seemed to not want a positive reply. Without letting me respond, she continued, tucking Lissy more securely in her seat and retrieving the cracker from her lap.

"How could you do that? And how could you treat a baby like Lissy was treated?"

I wondered what Tammy would think if she were to see the well-dressed woman who claimed maternity of this child, and who looked like she had never been neglected in her life. I knew that appearances were deceiving, and that most prostitutes became so as a result of abuses at home, but it was hard to imagine that Mava Melanson would not have wanted better for her children.

I left the foster home, content that Lissy was finally in the hands of someone who would care for her well. I wondered what her future would be, and realized that it was all in the hands of the court. Not a comforting thought when I thought of Tony's comments about fickle Lady Justice.

I had a few minutes to check in at the office before I went out to the Harper home. I had wanted to ask Mike something, but discovered that he was not in, which surprised me. I asked Tony, back at his desk catching up on his paperwork. He hesitated for a moment, and then said, "Mike has a rough time, He doesn't always make it in. We try to cover for him, okay?" his tone was between collusion and annoyance, and I wondered what was behind it, but decided to let it go. I'd ask Mike tomorrow.

There was also a message on my desk, on the pink paper that cheerily announced that while you were out, someone called. This one said, "Solander: baby boy, five pounds, two ounces. Premature but okay. St. John's Hospital. Mom wanted you to know." Well, well, so Gina had her baby after all! And almost a month early. I said a quick prayer that the baby was okay. What would she have done with a child with medical problems? She already had enough on her plate. I was pleased that we had apparently connected well enough for her to want me to know her news. I resolved to visit her tomorrow, if I could rearrange my schedule. Speaking of schedule, I had best get to the Harper's for my appointment.

Irene Harper lived in another section of the city that I would learn to know well. Populated by drug dealers and street people, the area was a haven for idealists who were bent on rehabilitation, a social worker paradise until one realized that the next group of new social workers would be working with the same people. There were a few families nestled amid the dysfunction. The rents were cheap, and that was a draw for those who needed inexpensive housing. Irene's home was a small bungalow that appeared to have been built along a driveway belonging to a duplex. It took me a while to discover this, despite the fact that the address, 55A, should have given me a clue. I parked my car on the street and walked up the driveway, not sure if the drive belonged to number 55 or to the Harpers.

The door was opened by a cute teenager who had a toddler saddled on her scant hip. The result was that the child kept slipping, requiring her to be hoisted and repositioned. I hoped that the teen did not hurt herself in the effort. The baby appeared to be a handful.

"You must be Terri," I greeted. She smiled, but remained a bit cautious. I introduced myself and the smile faded.

"Oh, Mom thought you were comin' tomorrow," she said quickly, hoisting the toddler once again.

"Is this Ellen?" I asked, trying to determine why Terri looked a bit ruffled. "Your Mom is not here?"

Terri hesitated. "No, but I could have her back here in a half an hour if you want to come back. She just forgot."

I found it interesting that a mother who was so intent upon the return of the rest of her children would forget when the social worker, who could give her that wish, came to visit. I decided that this one needed to be explored.

"Okay," I told her. "A half an hour it is. I'll be back."

As I got in my car, I noticed the curtain in the front window part and a face peeped out. Terri was apparently waiting until I left. For what? I cruised slowly down the street, keeping an eye on the house through my rearview mirror. I felt like someone out of a cheap detective novel and knew that I had to bone up on my surveillance skills. When I reached the end of the long block, I saw Terri emerge from the house with Ellen still glued tenuously to her hip. She looked around and then walked down the street hurriedly in the opposite direction. I watched until she turned a corner and disappeared. If I went around the block, I reasoned, I might be able to see her again. A right turn, and another found me driving slowly to the corner of the street onto which Terri had turned. I parked and looked up the street, thinking that if I was to do too much of this kind of thing, I had better invest in a car that was a bit less conspicuous than a red Volkswagen Bug.

My detective work was rewarded when Terri emerged from a doorway that I realized was that of a bar situated amidst the storefronts and private duplexes. The picture became clearer when I saw that she was almost dragging a woman who appeared a bit unsteady, obviously feeling the effects of her most recent stop. From her age and appearance, I guessed that this was Irene Harper, and that conscientious Terri intended to insure that appearances all looked good. Unsure of whether to confront them now or not, I sat in my car. The poor kid, I thought. Imagine wanting to be home with your Mom and knowing that she was about to blow it! I decided for Terri's sake, I would not fess up yet.

Half an hour later, I again knocked at the Harpers' door. Terri greeted me, and from the look on her face, I gathered that her attempts to sober her mother had failed.

"She's home," Terri told me. "She just really forgot. But we had a late night last night, see, and she is so tired. She came home and just fell into bed." Ellen toddled into the room with her fist full of cookies. Terri picked her up and again went through the hoist, slip, hoist routine.

"May I come in, Terri?" I asked gently. Her face fell. I am sure that she anticipated that her mother's reported exhaustion would be enough to send me off. I decided that I could no longer let her keep her secret. The court had returned her and her baby sister on the understanding that Irene Harper could be a fit mother. Being dragged from a bar by her teenage daughter did not get her the mother of the year award. I was the bad guy who had to answer to the court.

Terri stepped aside, and I entered a small living room furnished with old, not too stylish furniture that was probably collected from the Salvation Army. There was an attempt at cleanliness that I guessed was Terri's. Irene had apparently been bundled off to the bedroom. A cup of coffee, still warm, sat on the table in an adjoining room. I guessed that Terri had tried the black coffee remedy, to no avail. Terri gestured to the couch, and I sat, feeling like I didn't want to say what I had to say next.

"Terri, I saw you go and get her," I said, feeling the rush of emotion that traveled through the adolescent's body. "I'm really sorry. I know how much you wanted everything to look good." Terri's face was impassive, but huge tears began to streak her fair cheeks. Ellen reached up with a small hand still filled with cookies.

"Terri cryin'," she said in her baby voice. I felt like I had just delivered a death sentence. Then Terri began to sob, and as little Ellen put her arms around her, she buried her head in her sister's little body.

"I'm sorry, Terri," I said again, feeling so helpless.

"I thought I could make it work," she snuffled through her tears. "I was sure I could keep Mom off the booze. But I couldn't!" I guessed, rightly, I would learn, that this was not the first time that Irene Harper had left her children alone to answer the call of her addiction. I was to learn that Terri had skipped school several times to care for her baby sister while Irene slept off her latest binge.

"It wasn't up to you, Terri. No one can make another person stop drinking if they don't want to. Solving your Mom's problem was too much to be expected of you."

But her sobs continued, and I knew that my attempts at soothing her could not make up for the depth of her disappointment.

She hugged Ellen tighter.

"Do we have to go back to a foster home?" Terri asked weakly. Before I had a chance to answer, she cried, "Please don't separate Ellie and me again! Please! And I hated that last home. Not back there. Please!"

For years, we have been separating the oldest and youngest children in a large family. It has been a practice because we felt that the oldest, often the caretaker for younger siblings, needed the time and space to be a child. Often, the younger children were candidates for adoption, when their older siblings might be beyond the age that an adoption was easily possible. What we did not acknowledge was how much a part of the older child's feelings of worth caring for the littler ones had become, and how much that older child needed to maintain contact with the baby she had nurtured through so much. Terri brought this realization home for me in her one plea.

"I'll have to do some searching," I explained, "But I will see what I can do." I hoped that I was not getting her hopes up too high, only to disappoint her in the end. I also wondered what my superiors would say about breaching the accepted policy of separate placements. Where would I find a home that would take both a teenager and a toddler? Suddenly I thought of Tammy Howard, Lissy Melanson's caring foster mother. How many children had she been approved for? Six was the limit, and she had three of her own. With Lissy, Terri and Ellen, that would make six. But could she do it? Terri was not a behavior problem and would probably be a help with the little ones. As long as the foster mother was able to remain the authority figure and give Terri the chance to be a teen, it might work.

Normally, I should have taken both children with me after an attempt to talk to their mother. I had no doubt that the latter would be fruitless, and wondered if she could even be awakened. But Terri was fifteen and obviously responsible, and I was going down the street to find a phone that I could use in some degree of privacy from the ears of two anxious children. I made Terri promise that she would stay put, and hurried down the street to the phone not far from Irene's hangout, the bar. Mike had still not come in. The receptionist said that I should talk to the supervisor in the home-finding unit if I was looking for a foster home. Shortly, the supervisor, Maureen Daily, was on the phone and I explained the whole problem to her.

"It's a good, strong family," she told me, "But we don't want to burn them out. The Melanson child is their first one. I don't know," she was silent for a moment, and I sensed the intake and exhalation of breath that told me that she needed her cigarette to think.

"Okay, I'll tell you what," she finally concluded. "Let's let Tammy Howard make the decision if she can do it. But be sure to listen to the between the lines stuff. Like, if she thinks she needs to please you, like that. Let me know what happens."

"Thanks, Maureen, I will," I told her, and hung up, anxious to call the foster mother.

"Two?" Tammy said hesitantly, and my hopes were dashed. "Well, Lissy is doing well, and I love teenagers. We didn't apply to take them because I wasn't sure how I'd do with difficult problems. But you say this girl is a good kid, huh? The kids would love an older sister. And a three-year-old? That's a cute age. Is she up to par on her development? I am not sure I could handle two like Lissy." She thought again, and I was sure that she would say no. "Can I call you right back?" she asked. I explained that I was at a pay phone and suggested that I give her a few moments and call her back. We agreed, and I hung up wondering what to do if Tammy said no. I would call Maureen back, I guessed, and see what else they had. Maybe the two sisters could be placed in homes close to one another.

The seconds ticked by too slowly. I paced up and down the block, furtively eyeing the people who left the bar. It was now late afternoon, but I guessed by the look of some that they had spent the better part of the afternoon at the bar. I wondered what it would be like to have nothing better to do. A quick look at my watch. Ten minutes had dragged by. I waited another five and called Tammy back. She answered on the first ring, sounding much more excited than she had when we had last talked.

"I called Biff at work," she said referring to her husband. "He said we could do it. He can help if I need him, he told me. Okay! Let's do it!" There was none of the hesitation I had heard previously, and I felt sure that Tammy would be up to the task. I made arrangements to bring the girls to her, and I hung up with the feeling that things were looking up for Terri Harper and little Ellen.

If I expected things to be easy when I returned to the Harpers', I was mistaken. I was greeted by a hysterical Terri and a screaming Ellen.

"Help me! Help me!" Terri pleaded, running out to meet me. "She's cut her wrists! There's blood, come quick!"

I ran into the bathroom and found a woozy Irene Harper propped over the tub with wrists gaping and blood dripping into a pool on the white porcelain.

"Call 911!" I yelled back to Terri, who instantly became coherent.

"No phone!" she called back, and bolted out the door to the same phone I had used. Ellen watched her and screamed louder.

"Come here, honey," I coaxed, grabbing a towel and trying to wrap Irene's wrists. She resisted slightly and slumped over, apparently passed out. I hated to call Ellen into the room, but was afraid she would run after her sister. I laid Irene on the floor and prayed that the ambulance would be quick. Ellen had indeed toddled toward the door, and I scooped her up before she could go any further. She cried but didn't struggle, looking out the door and back to me.

"Terri will be right back," I comforted. It seemed an eternity before Terri came back, breathlessly.

"They're coming," she began, but the distant whir of sirens made her explanation unnecessary. Within minutes, the medics were at Irene's side and preparing to take her away to the hospital. A police officer questioned me and I assured him that I would be taking the children. He seemed relieved.

"A shame to have them witness this kind of thing!" he mumbled, shaking his head and getting back into his cruiser.

Terri was slumped on the couch, having calmed Ellen, but crying softly against the toddler.

"You okay?" I asked.

A new torrent of tears emerged from her already red eyes.

"It's my fault!" she wept. "It's all my fault! I didn't want to wait for you. I wanted to tell her myself. I was angry that she screwed up. I tried to wake her and tell her. I was angry. I shook her and yelled at her, 'they're taking us and it's all your fault!' But I thought she went back to sleep and then," her sobs prevented any more words.

"It's not your fault, Terri. I'm sorry. I shouldn't have left. I am so sorry," I wanted to cry too, as I wondered if this nightmare could have been prevented.

The remainder of the way to the Howards' I tried to help Terri to realize that her mother's suicide attempt was not her fault. The consequences of her and Ellen leaving were a direct result of Irene's inability to keep herself from drinking. By the time we reached the foster home, Terri had stopped crying and Ellen had fallen asleep on the back seat. Tammy's warmth soothed us all as she showed Terri around, and Biff, now home from work, carried a sleeping Ellen to a bed in the room that would be hers. I took Tammy aside and briefly explained the events of the afternoon. She was sympathetic, and promised to be sensitive to Terri's need to talk.

It was well after seven when I finally left the foster home, secure in the thought that Terri and Ellen were in capable hands. As I reviewed the events of the day, I realized that I too felt guilty about what had happened. I had made the decision to leave the house, albeit for a brief phone call. Had I left both Terri and Irene vulnerable?

It was something that I would think about for some time. As social workers, we cannot always make exactly the right decisions. Sometimes we have to learn to forgive ourselves for the decision that we made, thinking, at the time, that it was the best thing to do.

I forced my thoughts back to the present and realized that I had forgotten to call Maureen back. Under the circumstances, I thought that she would understand.

Questions for Thought

1. What are your impressions of juvenile court after reading this chapter?

2. What motivates an attorney to fight for the return of the child to Mava Melanson?

3. How might we reflect on the rights of children versus the rights of their parents?

4. How did you feel about Mike's problem? How would you have handled it had you been a worker in his unit?

5. What was your impression of Terri? What seems to motivate her?

6. How would you have handled the situation with Terri and her mother? Would you have left the house? How would you have felt after the incident?

7. What would have been the best plan for everyone?

19

A Mother's Legacy

Frequent calls over the next few weeks assured me that both Terri and Ellen had settled in well. Irene had been treated and released, and was now in another detox program. I wondered if having lost her children for the third time would inspire her to finally kick her habit. Only time would tell. I wondered if the court would give her another chance, or if the judge would order permanent custody of the children to the Department. With such an order, we could then petition to have them released for adoption. I wasn't sure who that would really benefit, however. Perhaps Ellen would be a good candidate for adoption, but her attachment to Terri would make that difficult. Maybe nine-year-old Paul might adjust to an adoptive home, but he was in foster care with his older brothers Eddie and Howie. I doubted that an adoptive couple could be found for the sibling group, especially when Howie had become such a handful.

Today, the horizon might have been much brighter for Irene Harper's children. Not only is open adoption more widely used, but adoption units are more likely to search for couples that will take older children and sibling groups. At that time, a five-year-old was considered to be an older child, and the likelihood of the Harper siblings being able to maintain contact would have been slim.

The Harpers were on my mind several months later when I set my morning coffee on my desk and surveyed the myriad of pink phone messages that awaited me. Three of the six were from the Harper boys' foster mother, Cloe Cummings. "Urgent!" the last one read. Oh, great! Now what? I had been to see the boys in their foster home on several occasions. Mrs. Cummings struck me as a bit of a worrywart, but the boys seemed to like her well enough. Howie was still on probation after stealing a neighbor's car, and he saw his probation officer on a regular basis. He was also the least likable of the brothers. Paul at nine was timid and self-conscious. He and Eddie were as light as Terri and Howie were dark, attesting the Irene's changing tastes in husbands. Eddie was a daredevil, but not a bad kid if you could keep up with him. The foster mother suggested that we might have him tested for Attention Deficit Hyperactivity Disorder, but I didn't think he was any more than just a very active boy. But

I promised her the evaluation just to be sure. Howie, dark and sullen, seemed to slink around the house. Mrs. Cummings described him as having a sneaky streak that concerned her. She was a competent and caring foster mother, and I believe that she really tried to like Howie, but I suspected that he didn't like anyone, especially himself. There were questions in earlier dictation of Fetal Alcohol Syndrome, but more recently those had been discounted. I suspected that Irene Harper, chained to the demands of her addiction, had had little time for her infant son, hampering his ability to bond with anyone in later life.

Now we recognize that this inability to bond is common among foster children who were born to parents who could not care for themselves, let alone their offspring. Termed Attachment Disorder, I had seen it in Jessica Barton when I was in the adoption unit and knew that foster care abounded with such children. These children never quite connected with anyone, and often bounced from placement to placement. New therapies are now being tried to reach the seemingly unreachable, but we knew little of this disorder at that time. We were not aware of the importance of consistency in addressing these children's needs, and we allowed them to be moved from place to place. I hoped that Mrs. Cummings was not asking for Howie's removal.

Cloe Cummings answered the phone in her usual efficient manner. Before deciding to become a foster mother, she had worked as an executive secretary, and I had no doubt that she had fulfilled her role well. She was organized and efficient, but this was tempered with friendly manner that made her entirely approachable. But when she discovered that it was me, her manner changed.

"I really need to talk with you," she said, as close to losing her cool as I had ever heard. "Howie sexually assaulted Paul. We don't know what to do! I just can't have him here!" she was close to tears. I assured her that I could come out later in the day, and she felt that she could hold on until then. Her husband Fred, who ran his own repair business, had taken Howie to work with him, as they did not want to send him to school with the other children. In the meantime, they had been trying to reach me. I wondered why I had not been notified at home last night, and went in search of Mike to find out.

"He's out again," my colleague Donna told me, rolling her eyes in the manner that she used often to show disapproval.

"Again? Why?" I asked. Mike was often out and there was rarely a good explanation that I heard.

"Same old thing!" she quipped, and went off, apparently expecting me to know what she meant.

Tony walked by and was the nearest target for my annoyance.

"What is going on? I need to run a case by Mike, a possible removal and a sexual abuse situation, and he's nowhere around. Where the heck is he?"

Tony stopped and looked at me with concern.

"You don't know?" he asked in a low voice.

"Know what?" I said loudly, in no mood to play secrecy games.

"Shhh! Come 'ere." He pulled me over to one side of the office where no one appeared to be about.

"Mike has this, ah, little problem. We all know about it and try to help him out," he explained.

"What little problem?"

"Well, he kinda bends the elbow too much, you know?" He gestured taking a drink and I began to understand.

"Mike's an alcoholic?"

"I suppose you could say that. We just think of it as hitting the sauce a little heavy, but, yeah, you could say that. We try to cover for him when he has his little problem, so he doesn't get fired," Tony continued, assuming that I would go along.

It explained a great deal that had been going on over the last few months. Mike's frequent absences, his headaches some mornings, his long lunches that I had already suspected were taken at a local Irish pub. I would also learn in my years with the Department that alcoholism was not unusual among protective workers. The work was tough, it played on your emotions, and the need to play hard seemed an appropriate response. I had been to a few of the after-hours parties, and had found them too loud, rough, and the booze flowing too freely for my taste. I did not consider myself a prude, but I preferred my addictions to be less lethal. Chocolate and work were enough for me.

I felt badly for Mike, but there was nothing that I could do about his problem right now. I needed some help.

"Who has the authority to authorize a move if Mike is not here? My guess is that the foster mother won't want to keep this kid," I filled Tony in on the conversation with Cloe Cummings. He already knew a bit about the case, although not the latest events. Each member of the unit had an idea about the cases of his or her coworkers in case an emergency necessitated coverage by a colleague.

"My guess is that this kid needs residential," Tony concluded. "Not too many foster homes are going to take a budding sex offender." He told me to speak with the supervisor who covered for Mike in his absence. The supervisor agreed that I should have a plan when I went out to the foster home, and put me in touch with the Residential Services Unit.

The Residential Services Unit coordinated the placements of children in residential settings. Children who were unable, for one reason or another, to remain in the family setting of foster care, often benefited from a placement in one of the many residential settings throughout the state. Serving every type of need from mental retardation and medical problems to emotional disturbance, autism, and Fetal Alcohol Syndrome, these centers varied from large institutions to small group homes. There were even a few who would consider taking children who were acting out sexually. When a child was referred to the unit, his or her case was reviewed to determine the type of need. Each Residential Services worker oversaw a number of residential placements and knew the policies well. Once placed, the child would become mostly the responsibility of the Residential Services (RS) worker who kept in touch with the family's social worker. I had never worked with an RS worker, but I knew that the success of the arrangement depended largely on the RS worker to whom your child was assigned. The Residential Services supervisor promised to review Howie's case quickly and be ready with a suggestion when I called in from the foster home. It was a back-up plan, as I had no idea if Mrs. Cummings would actually want Howie placed. But from her tone on the phone, I guessed that the back-up plan might be needed.

The Cummings' foster home was an attractive ranch that testified to Mr. Cummings' ability to fix things. Everything seemed to be efficiently patched, from the picket fence to the front steps. The yard also housed an array of spare parts, from old engines to wooden planks and boxes of assorted pieces that were apparently destined to fix something at some time. But unlike many similar houses, the parts were neatly arranged and, as Mrs. Cummings once told me, catalogued so that they might be easily found. Such organization amazed me. I was lucky if I could find things in my somewhat cluttered room, let alone catalogue them.

Cloe Cummings greeted me, still seeming a bit flustered. She said that she had kept Paul home and he was sleeping at the moment.

"Poor Paulie," she said in sympathy. "He is so upset. He was lying in bed crying last night. I finally got out of him that Howie had threatened him with one of my kitchen knives. Howie told Paulie he'd kill him unless he agree to let him do sexual stuff to him."

"What type of stuff?" I asked, knowing that I would have to include this in my report. I knew that the foster mother was uncomfortable, but it couldn't be helped.

Hesitantly, she continued, "He wanted Paulie to touch him and to let him put his penis in Paulie's bum. Paulie was so upset."

"Where was Eddie during all this?"

"Fred had taken him to the repair shop with him. It's kind of a treat for each of the boys to go with him separately from time to time. Paul wasn't feeling well, so he went to bed early. Howie said he'd like to turn in early too, and I thought nothing of it." She was wringing her hands in a manner so uncharacteristic of this usually together woman.

"I heard Paulie crying, and I went in. Howie appeared to be asleep. Paul clung to me and said, 'Couldn't he go into the guest room?' Sometimes when one of the kids is sick, we let them go in there so the others don't catch anything. So I took him in there and he started crying harder and told me what had happened. I was so upset. Paul was petrified of his brother, so I let him stay in the guest room. When Fred came home, I told him. He was ready to go in and throttle Howie. He put Eddie in the guest room with Paul and said he would deal with Howie in the morning. He calmed down before he went off with him, but I don't imagine that Howie has had a really pleasant day." She seemed out of breath as she finished her narrative.

"Has it happened before?" I asked.

"I thought of that. I asked Paul and he said that his brother had been touching him sometimes, but he had never forced him or threatened him like last night. To think it was going on in my own house and I didn't even know it," she began to cry. "Whatever would have made Howie do it?"

I explained that when children were abused, they might act out their abuse on younger children. A perusal of the Harper record had told me that there was a suspicion that Howie's father may have abused him sexually, but nothing had been confirmed. I suspected now that it had been true. I told the concerned foster mother about my finding.

"I just can't keep him," she told me tearfully. I told her that I needed to talk to Paul, and later Howie, but that I had been exploring other arrangements for the disturbed boy. She seemed relieved and told me that she would see if Paul was awake. She didn't think that he had slept well last night, and was quite tired.

In a few moments, the foster mother reappeared with a sleepy boy. She left us alone, feeling that Paul might be more comfortable. His story was pretty much like hers, though he admitted that Howie had threatened him before, but not with a knife or any other type of weapon. I talked with Paul about his fear, and explained that Howie might be going away to get some help. I assured Paul that it was not his fault, and that the problem was Howie's. The waif-like blonde boy nodded, and seemed to accept that he would be safe from further abuse.

I put in a call to the Residential Services Unit and found that they had arranged for a placement for Howie in a residential setting that dealt with children who were acting out sexually. The placement had been arranged for the next day.

"Would you like to have us place Howie overnight?" I asked when I explained the arrangements to the foster mother.

"No, I think we can handle things tonight," she assured me, adopting some of her previous take-charge manner.

Mrs. Cummings called her husband's shop and arranged for me to talk with Howie in a back office of the business. He was his usual sullen self, neither admitting nor denying the abuse of his brother. I explained that I would be seeking a placement where he could get some help and Howie's face remained impassive. Did he like being with the Cummings? One would never know from his affect. As I was about to end the interview, he mumbled something under his breath that I was not sure I had heard at first. His tone disturbed me as much as the words. It was vengeful and filled with rage. As I thought more about it, I realized what he had said. In a voice filled with malice, he had mumbled, "He had it coming!"

As I returned to the office to finalize the arrangements with the RSU and fill out the paperwork that would transfer Howie to the Hillcrest School for Boys, I thought of the legacy that Irene Harper had left to her children. Neglected, unloved, abandoned, sexually abused, and made to be a parent to their drunken mother, Irene's five children had suffered more than any child should. We knew little about Irene's own background. I wondered if she, too, had endured the kind of childhood her children were living. Maybe I was being too hard on her. Was hers merely a story without end, of a mother who never learned to mother because she was never cared for in childhood? Had alcohol become this mother's escape from a life that she did not want to remember and the responsibilities that she was unable to face? I hoped that the cycle of violence, neglect, and abuse could be broken for at least some of her children.

Questions for Thought

1. How do you think the case of Irene Harper should have been resolved? Should the mother have been given another chance?

2. How would you have felt answering Cloe Cummings' call? What might you have said to her? How would you have handled the case?

3. Would you have left Howie at the Cummings' overnight?

4. What might the Cummings have been feeling? What might Howie have been feeling? What about his brothers?

20

A Transfer to the Front Lines

I had been in protective services for close to a year when the offer came to join the Intake Unit. Herb, my constant supporter, urged me to take the transfer.

"Your unit doesn't need to be a soap opera," he told me. "You get enough excitement with your cases!"

I was tiring of covering up for Mike, who seemed to be slipping deeper and deeper into his own problems. Tony mentioned that his wife was threatening to divorce him, driving Mike further into his liquid escape. Even though the two men had been friends for a long time, I think that Tony was also feeling the strain. Sure that Mike's days as supervisor were numbered if things continued as they were, I think that Tony was also looking for a move. So it was that both Tony and I transferred to Intake under the supervision of Polly Stern, a no-nonsense woman in her late forties. Due to the fact that Mike's unit had just become shorthanded, I agreed to keep some of my ongoing cases including Gina's, the Harpers', and the Melanson's.

The legal custody of Star Whitedeer had been given to the Department after numerous attempts at enlisting her mother's cooperation had failed. I felt badly, as I knew that Native Americans often showed their protest by silence. It was the age-old problem of how to explain to someone from another culture that the laws of the land must be obeyed, regardless of cultural mores. If Dawn Whitedeer would not help to gain her child's return, there was nothing that we could do but remove her permanently. Star's case had been referred to the adoption unit and a petition had been filed in Probate court to release her for adoption. Now we just waited for the legal wheels to turn.

The Melanson case still dragged on. The criminal case against Mava Melanson had been continued once again, leaving the juvenile court case still in limbo. In the meantime, Lissy was being well cared for by Tammy Howard with some input from Terri Harper.

I had visited Howie several times in his residential home. After a rough start, he was doing better. His younger brothers seemed to be flourishing with the Cummings, and I had finally gotten approval for Paul to see a therapist to evaluate if the sexual abuse by his older brother had affected him emotionally.

Once or twice a week, there was a call from Gina. She and the new baby, Garth, had come home soon after I visited them in the hospital. The baby had gained weight quickly, and appeared not to have been too traumatized by his premature birth. Although Gina seemed happy to be a new mother again, the situation with Betty Jane still concerned her. I had petitioned to have the judge mandate that Trudy's visits with her daughter be supervised, as we suspected sexual abuse. But the ruling came back that we had no proof that the abuse was current. The whole unit of social workers could not believe that decision, and Mike had suggested that I refer the case to the Department attorney. Gina had tried to invent reasons why Betty could not go when it was her mother's time to visit, but Trudy's attorney called and complained. So, while we tried to make the wheels of justice turn for the best interests of little Betty Jane, she continued to have unsupervised visits with her mother. Finally, our attorney engineered a turn in the decision, and I had to bring Betty Jane to the office every other week for Trudy to have her visit there. It did not surprise me that Trudy was angry about this arrangement and did everything in her power to be objectionable.

As I sat behind the one-way mirror observing the visit one day, I thought how much some people sacrifice their children's needs to get back at other adults. It seemed obvious from the interchange between the large, mannish woman and the less than enthusiastic child, that Trudy had little real interest in her daughter. Rather, she seemed to push the visits as a way of annoying Gina and Rudy. Now, she read a magazine while Betty Jane played with some dolls on the floor of the playroom. There was little interaction between mother and child, and the visits always made me feel somehow hollow. What a contrast this mother was to the gentle, creative Gina, who always found some way to interact with the children.

I also visited with Gina from time to time, listening to her tales of the children's activities and admiring the latest picture she had drawn. I was so impressed by her talent that I had given her a drawing pad and charcoal, which she treated with utmost care. Mirroring my interest, perhaps, she took much more pride in her pictures, and they were now hung among the children's drawings on the refrigerator and the walls. I enjoyed our visits, too mindful of the fact that the case should probably have been closed, as the children in question were being well cared for. However, while there was still a possibility of abuse, even if it was on visits with the mother, we had to keep the case open. Despite the fact that there were now supervised visits, Trudy was trying to appeal the decision. We hoped that somehow justice would finally come through for the best interests of Betty Jane.

The Intake office was away from the others, probably due to the fact that there were always phones ringing and often confusion. Tony's and my desk were next to each other, and the desks of the three other workers in the unit were on the opposite side of the room. The luxury of the Intake Unit, and possibly the only one, was that you had your own phone. If a worker was not on duty answering the phone that day, he or she was calling back collaterals, those people interested in a case but not directly involved, or checking out facts. At that time, we took an intake call and were assigned the case through the screening and assessment. It was the Intake worker's job to determine if there was reason to believe that abuse or neglect was occurring, investigate, and come up with a treatment plan. More recently, the functions of intake and assessment have become separate, with different workers doing the separate functions. But we had the whole front end of the case then, and I was to learn that it could be a bit of a challenge.

Each of us spent two days on call every week, meaning that there were always two of us to cover Intake. This was important, since the office always had to be covered, leaving one person to go out on emergency if necessary. I enjoyed working with Tony and Dana the most. Dana was a slight man about my age. He always had a unique way of looking at things, and kept us chuckling in our downtime. Tony had become a friend and confidant, and we shared some good times together. In Intake, you started the day with coffee and a donut, not knowing when or if you would have time to eat again. Of course, one began the day with an obligatory check of the non-emergency phone messages that had come in.

There was usually a newspaper that you could peruse if things had not already gotten busy. In addition to keeping us up on current events, a newspaper often furnished us with glimpses into what was to come. A marital dispute worth reporting, for example, usually meant that we may well be called to find a place for the children while Mom was hospitalized and Dad dragged off by the police. And it was not uncommon to read about a fire burning out multiple families, and then discover that it was up to us to help with the homeless children.

I had not had a chance to see the paper that morning when I hurried into the office, hoping that Polly did not realize that I was late. A workaholic herself, my new supervisor expected everyone else to adopt this style as well, quite a change from the relaxed and somewhat inconstant manner of Mike. Our unit meetings took place like clockwork, not only because it was necessary to keep up to date on cases in Intake, but also due to Polly's idea of a well-run unit.

"Whew, will you look at this!" said Dana, my colleague for the day, although Tony and another worker had come in to catch up on calls and paperwork.

" 'Woman brutally slays lesbian lover'," he read the headline with dramatic emphasis. "Anyone we know?"

"Not me," chimed in Tony. "All my lesbian lovers are still living."

Dana began to read aloud, "Police received a call from a hysterical neighbor last night after she had found the corpse of a woman beaten to death in the alley behind her home. The corpse has been identified as forty-year-old Trudy Kaplan of 782 Forrest Ave."

I had been only half listening, but the familiar name snapped me to attention.

"What? Let me see that!" I grabbed the paper from Dana, who looked surprised.

"Police believe that the woman was murdered by her live-in lesbian lover, Jane DeMoira of the same address. Ms. DeMoira was apprehended several hours after the body was found, and has been arrested. Oh my gosh!" I heard myself utter.

"Your case?" Tony asked, as he came over to my desk. He had heard me complain about the visits and had obviously put together the pieces.

It was the first of the two times in my career that one of my clients was murdered, and the feelings it generated are difficult to describe. Perhaps anyone who has just seen a person killed violently will attest to the myriad of emotions that surge through your body. Certainly I had no love for Betty Jane's mother, who had been especially difficult during her supervised visit two days before, but I did not wish her to come to this end. I thought of Betty and Mercy, and wondered how it would affect them. I wondered if they even knew. Calming myself, knowing that there was a job to be done, I called Gina.

"Do the girls," I started to blurt out but Gina interrupted.

"We know about Trudy," she said quietly. I guessed that the girls had not yet gone to school, or perhaps Gina intended to keep them home today. "Rudy got a paper on the way to work. He called us. The girls are here with me now."

"How are they?" I asked, realizing that it might be hard for her to talk.

"Pretty good, considering," she told me.

"Should I come over?" Betty Jane and I especially had developed a close relationship, as I brought her to the office for her visits. We often got an ice cream on the way home, and I had grown to like the little girl.

"Maybe not now. Give us some time. Later, maybe." Gina seemed to be in perfect control, and I realized that wanting to dash over there might be satisfying my own need rather than the family's. I told her that I would be over later, hoping that I would not be called out on a case, and that someone would agree to cover for me in the office. Workers understood how the unexpected could come up, and were good about covering for one another.

As I sat at my desk, having been consoled by my coworkers, I hoped that no calls would come in that morning. I needed time to think. No sooner had I had this thought when the phone rang. I looked around for Dana, but he was talking with Polly in her office and obviously expected me to answer it.

"Is this the child protection people?" a deep female voice asked urgently.

When I assured her that it was, she went on.

"I have Tommy here with me. He's been beat somethin' bad. He ain't goin' back to that fuckin' bitch while there's a bone in my body! You haveta' come get him."

I urged her to tell me the whole story, and she was able to explain that Barbara Schwartz, the neighbor upstairs, lost her temper with her six children and beat them regularly.

"And she leaves them alone, too. I've heard those babies cryin' and she's gone off somewhere. It happens all the time. She took off after Tommy came down here to me, and I haven't seen her since. That was an hour ago. I'll just bet those babies are alone up there! I know you people have been out here before, a couple of years ago. Don't know why ya done nothing then!"

Since it was quite possible that Tommy needed medical attention and there was a chance that young children were left alone, I knew that I had to go out on it. I collected all the information that the caller had to offer, and told her that I would be there within the hour.

"You just better hurry!" she ordered, before we broke the connection.

Since the caller had said that the case was known to us, I asked the secretary to search the files while I got ready to go out. I let Dana know that I had to go out on a call, and checked with the secretary who said that Schwartz had been an open case several years ago when our office had been called in by the local hospital, who said that four-year-old Tommy had been brought to the emergency room after swallowing drain cleaner. He was admitted, and underwent surgery to repair the extensive burning that had been done by the substance. The hospital suggested that he might have been forced to take the drain cleaner, but after an extensive investigation, no proof could be established. The case was followed for several months after the child's release. The record noted that the mother's housekeeping was barely within acceptable standards, but efforts to work with the mother caused an improvement. The case was finally closed.

Now having some idea of what I was facing, I picked up my purse and left the office. The clouds above threatened rain, and I remembered that we'd been promised a significant storm. I hoped the weatherman would live up to his usual reputation and be wrong.

I followed the directions given by the caller and found myself in front of an old building that housed about eight apartments. The caller was a large, grandmotherly woman with flaming red hair that could not have been a product of nature. She ushered me into her living room and introduced herself as Freda Francis. Tommy cowered when he saw me, and I wondered what he had been told about social workers. The lower part of his face around his mouth was badly disfigured, with scar tissue of various colors. I cringed to think that anyone could be guilty of doing this to a child. I preferred to imagine that it had been an accident. I tried to soothe Tommy enough to look at his wounds. In fact, he was bruised about his neck and shoulders. There was also a rope burn around his leg, usually caused by someone hitting a child with a belt, robe, cord, or other long, thin object. There was a bald spot on Tommy's head, and I guessed that he had been grabbed by his hair.

I tried to explain to the child that I'd like to take him to the emergency room to make sure he had no internal injuries. He began to cry, and shook his head vigorously. The effort obviously caused pain, and Freda Francis sat him on the couch and talked to him softly. He calmed, and I guessed that he had spent quite a bit of time at the neighbor's house.

"Can I go wit' youse?" she asked. "He'd like that."

I agreed that she could accompany us, and while she was getting ready, I went upstairs to the Schwartz apartment. Several knocks produced no response, and I contemplated what to do when the door was finally opened a crack. The child who poked her face out could have been no more than ten or eleven.

"What?" she said in a tone that let me know that she was in charge.

"Is Mommy home?"

"She's busy!"

"I need to speak with her," I told the small, disheveled child. I told her who I was, and that I must speak to her Mommy. She panicked when she heard who I was, and tried to slam the door. A well-placed foot prevented her.

"Your Mommy isn't home, right?" at that she seemed to crumble. She started crying and backed away from the door, letting it swing open. The stench was the first thing that hit me. Bits of food rotting in corners, garbage overflowing and not recently emptied, animal excrement, and dirty diapers combined to produce a collage of odors that was enough to make the strongest stomach wretch. Three children, all under eight years old, were huddled on a soiled mattress in one bedroom. A baby lay listlessly in a crib with a long ago curdled bottle at his side. The apartment was furnished, but the covers on the chairs and couch were tattered and very dirty. Several cats skittered into corners, looking as much in need of a good meal as their human owners.

"Mom's gone out!" the oldest child told me, recovering her composure briefly.

"How long ago?"

" 'Coupla hours," was her innocent reply.

"Is there any adult here with you?" She shook her head, eyeing me suspiciously.

Technically, the children were considered abandoned and should be taken into custody, but I knew that there was no way that I could fit six children and the helpful Freda into my Volkswagen Bug. I asked the oldest girl if she had a phone, and she pointed silently to an object on the table that was partially covered with clothes. I unearthed the old telephone and gingerly dialed for police backup. Police officers were often used when children had to be removed from a home. Their presence also helped if an irate parent came on the scene just as you were bundling the children up in the car or cruiser. I also put in a call to a crisis foster home, a family that had agreed to take children temporarily in this type of situation. Sure that help would soon be on the way, I returned to the children to soothe them and try to let them know what was happening. They were obviously frightened, which was not surprising.

Within an hour, I had taken Tommy and Freda Francis to the hospital, where the child was admitted for further observation. Freda asked if she could stay until the mother was contacted. The police had transported the children to an emergency foster home. Now to get a court order.

Whenever a social worker was forced to remove children from a home, he or she was required to secure an order from the court as soon as possible. The clerk of court was sympathetic.

"Schwartz! I've heard that name before!" he said, as he handed me the paperwork. "Good luck!"

I returned to the office to be faced with an irate call from Barbara Schwartz.

"What the hell have you done with my kids?" she stormed. I gave her several minutes to fume and rage and use every word in her rather limited vocabulary. Then I suggested that she come to the office, and I would explain the whole thing. After a few more splutters she yelled, "You bet I will!" and the phone crashed in my ear. I prepared for the onslaught of an enraged parent as I took several other calls.

I busied myself in the office, taking calls and doing paperwork. A call came in from a woman who said that she had her two nieces and a nephew and wondered how she could place them in the care of the Department since their mother, her sister, had died and she felt that their father was unfit. I told her that that would be difficult without proving that he was unfit. If she felt that there was evidence of his inability to parent, she could apply for guardianship herself in probate court.

"Oh, no. You don't understand," she said. "You don't know Morris, the children's father! I couldn't get custody myself. I need help."

I suggested that she come to the office to speak to me the next day, since she assured me that the story was too complicated to recount over the phone.

By 4:00, Barbara Schwartz had not appeared, and I wondered if she would. But at four fifteen, the secretary alerted me that I had a client to see me. I am not sure what I expected in Barbara Schwartz after our phone conversation, but it was not the woman I saw. What sounded like a burly trucker ready to do battle, turned out to be a petite, frail-looking woman who hardly looked old enough to have six children. She, like her children, was thin and malnourished, with deep circles under her gray eyes.

I ushered her into a meeting room and immediately she began to cry.

"I can't do it! I just can't do it," she wailed. "I love my babies! I really do!" At this point, she began to blurt out her whole life story in bits and pieces between sobs. I was able to piece together a fairly coherent picture.

Born on a farm in Ohio, she had married young and followed her husband to the east coast, where he promptly left her with one baby and another on the way. She received welfare for several years and had several relationships, producing three more babies. Six years ago, she had taken up with Bart, and they moved into the apartment where she now lived. He was a drug dealer, and hooked Barbara on drugs. Bart also beat the children, and she felt powerless to stop him or was so strung out that she was not even aware of what was happening. He especially disliked Tommy, and in a fit of anger forced him to drink the drain cleaner. After a particularly violent fight, Bart left and has not returned in two years. When Barbara no longer had a drug supplier, she began to shoplift to support her habit. A year ago, she had been arrested and sent to a drug rehabilitation program while she farmed her children out to relatives. But when she went back on drugs several months later, the relatives told her she was on her own. She did not say how she was supporting her habit, but I suspected that she was prostituting for money or drugs.

"I hate how I feel!" she wailed. "I'm sick all the time. Please help me!"

Despite her story about her children being beaten by a boyfriend, there was still little Tommy, spending the night in the hospital with obvious bruises.

"And what about Tommy? What happened to him?" Barbara's slender face whitened.

"I don't know what happens to me sometimes. When my Daddy used to beat the crap out of me, I vowed I'd never do that to my kids, but," she broke into sobs again.

It was so unusual for an abuser, let alone a drug abuser, to actually be asking for help that I was encouraged. We talked about how her children could remain in foster care while she once again checked herself into a five-day rehab program. After that, she would be supervised carefully while getting herself back on her feet. Since there had been a court order authorizing the removal of her children and there would be a hearing to follow, she would have to prove that she could care for them before the children could be returned. Barbara agreed tearfully, and we completed the necessary paperwork.

Barbara Schwartz was another client who taught me a great deal about the strength of the human spirit. She completed rehab, and her children were eventually returned. I followed the case for a short period of time and discovered in her a woman who really wanted to parent. She had a tough time, slipping back into her addiction from time to time, but she would always get herself back into detox again. Never a good housekeeper, Barbara finally managed to maintain acceptable standards, possibly because she began to want desperately to please me. Months later, I would visit her inner city apartment to discover that it had been cleaned of as many layers of the accumulated dirt as possible. The smell was nothing like what had assaulted me that first morning. And on the kitchen table where we sat to talk was a huge bouquet of lilacs. I thought it best not to ask about their origin, considering that the only vegetation I was aware of was in the city park several blocks away, and picking was prohibited. The fact that I am very allergic to lilacs was something that I would never tell Barbara, so I spent our interview with a wad of tissues, apologizing for the terrible cold I had, comforted by the effort that she was finally making to demonstrate her improvement. From that visit, which I recounted in great detail when I returned to the office, my coworkers came up with the adage, "one must look for the flowers amidst the filth" to help us focus on a client's strengths rather than her or his weaknesses.

Questions for Thought

1. How do you feel about the resolution of the Whitedeer case? How much must we take into consideration the cultural practices of others? Should those with different cultural practices be required to meet the criteria set for others?

2. How do you feel about the outcome of Betty Jane's case?

3. What might be your feelings about transferring into the Intake Unit?

4. What would have been your feelings about the Schwartz case?

5. Would you have handled the Schwartz case differently?

21

Childhoods in Hell

Valerie Anderson was an attractive brunette who was anxious to tell me her story. She sat across from me in the small office meeting room and looked quite concerned.

"The children are doing well now. They were so upset when they came. Denise was a good mother, but they had to watch her die, and that couldn't have been easy for them."

I had heard bits and pieces of the woman's incredible story, but I felt as if the fragments could not possibly be fit together to reveal the picture that I had in my mind. I suggested, therefore, that she tell me the whole story.

Denise Farley, Valerie's younger sister, had been living with her husband, Morris, and their three children in Maine. Valerie described her brother-in-law as an "egotistical idiot who thought only of himself and money." When Denise was diagnosed with cancer and had to quit her job, Morris decided that the family was spending too much money. He moved his small brood to what Valerie told me could only be described a shack in the woods. A successful, self-employed accountant, Morris did not feel that they needed medical insurance, and so the family had none. So, explained the grieving sister, Morris continued to don his expensive suit and speed off to work in his Jaguar while his wife was left to die a painful death with only her small children for company. The family, from whom Morris had kept Denise since they were married, knew nothing of this. But after Denise's death, Morris, needing help with the children, brought them to Valerie, asking if she would keep them while he tried to find office space in the area. It was only after the children's various comments that Valerie was able to piece together the unbelievable story.

"I can't give them back to that monster!" she said with vehemence. "What can I do? I'll be glad to keep them. My husband and I have only one daughter and we can certainly keep the children. I am not even sure why Morris wants them, except he treats them like his little slaves. They are made to wait on him hand and foot."

"Why haven't you just gotten guardianship?" I asked, wondering why she had enlisted our help.

Valerie Anderson paused and looked at me thoughtfully. "You don't know Morris. I guess I am a little afraid of him," she admitted quietly.

I told her that I would have to see Morris and we would then determine what would be in the best interest of the children. From her story, it sounded as though her home might be the appropriate place for them, but I could make no promises.

As she was leaving, Valerie Anderson hesitated, as if something else had occurred to her.

"He was treated in a clinic in Maine. The children said they thought it was because he was depressed, but I wonder. I think it was the mental health center in Portland. You might want to check it out."

Back in the office, I thought about the case. I could not imagine what it must have been like for Denise Farley to die slowly, without medical attention, while her children looked on. Was Morris really the monster that Valerie described him to be?

"You have a call," Tony told me, as I sat wondering how next to proceed in this strange case.

Gina's cheerful voice greeted me as I took the call, and I was thankful for her breath of sunshine in an otherwise cloudy day.

"Guess what!" she chirped.

"I can't imagine."

"I'm pregnant!" I could not believe her joyful tone as I thought of her apartment already filled with six children. I wanted to appear enthused and congratulate her, but my heart was not in it. Could she really handle one more? I finally managed what I hoped sounded like a cheerful congratulation. But Gina was not finished with her news.

"And Rudy's daughter Michelle, the one who is seventeen, wants to move in for a while. She was living with her boyfriend, but he's been beating her up and Rudy thinks she should leave him. So we said she could come here until she finds another place."

I groaned inwardly, and trying not to burst her bubble too much, said, "Are you sure you can manage with all those people, Gina?"

"Oh, sure. We'll be fine." I was glad that she was optimistic. "Michelle will be a big help with the kids."

Feeling in need of another, more realistic, positive report, I called Tammy Howard, the foster mother who I checked with periodically. I had not been out recently due to an overwhelming intake schedule, and I wanted to make sure that she was okay.

Tammy was her usual cheerful self, making me feel that the world could not be as dark as it sometimes seemed.

"Lissy is walking! Isn't that great?"

Now, that was a piece of news that I could really get excited about. The progress that Tammy had made with that child was incredible. Lissy had thinned down on a healthy diet, and had responded well to the stimulation that Terri Harper and Ellen had brought to the home. It was heartwarming to visit, and I decided that I owed myself the treat of visiting soon.

Resigned to the fact that after the shot of optimism I had gotten from Tammy I must return to less inspiring cases, I put in a call to the mental health clinic in Maine. I knew that they could not tell me much without a release from Morris Farley, but I figured that I might learn something. The therapist who had treated Farley was not in, but I left my name, with the request that he return my call. Since it was Friday, I guessed that I would not hear until the beginning of the week. In the meantime, I hoped that the Farley children would be okay at their aunt's. Valerie had also given me Morris' number at the office so that I could contact him. She was also nervous that when he discovered we were involved, he would suspect that his children might not be returned to him. Since she was sure that he would be really angry and was fearful of his anger, I decided to wait until Monday to contact him as well.

The rest of the afternoon was relatively uneventful. As 4:30 rolled around, I realized how long half an hour could seem. I looked forward to the weekend, knowing that Herb and I had plans to go away. I could use the rest.

When the phone rang at 4:50, both Tony, who was my partner that day, and I looked at it mournfully. I finally grabbed it and Tony smiled an "I owe you one" smile.

"Hello," said a young voice. "Do you place kids in jail?"

"What do you mean?" I asked, with a puzzled look in Tony's direction.

"I need to go to jail. I just did something really bad."

"Tell me your name," I said, trying to be reassuring. I didn't want to lose this call. "And what you did."

"It's Sam. And I killed my Mommy."

Now my senses were alert and Tony, seeing my change in posture, was there with pen and paper to take any directions I might give.

"How old are you, Sam?"

"Eight," came the reply.

I also got the child to give me his address, and I jotted it down for Tony, who knew what to do. On the other phone, he quickly dialed the police who would be there, we hoped, in minutes. I explained to him that the police were coming, and that he was to let the police in when they came. It was difficult to explain that they were coming to help rather than to drag him off to jail, but I tried. Until we knew what had really happened, we could only give him vague reassurances. I also told the child that I would be there as soon as I could, and to tell the police that.

It was 5:00 as I hurriedly got my things together to go out on the call.

"Why does everything always happen on Friday afternoon?" I said to Tony. He laughed and shrugged. I called Herb to tell him I'd be late. He was sympathetic, having worked once in Protective Services before he "retired to adoption," as he put it.

Tony watched me thoughtfully, and as if finally resigning himself, he sighed deeply.

"I'll come with you on this one," he said, grabbing his coat. "You might need help. And furthermore," he chuckled again, "my wife wants me to help her clean the basement. I'd rather do this!" I rolled my eyes in his direction, knowing that he would much prefer to be home, but thankful for his company.

Police cars were already at the scene when we arrived and an ambulance was just about to take the body away. A stocky officer with whom I had worked before approached us.

"Hi Chuck," Tony greeted him with a familiarity that made me suspect that this was one more guy from the old neighborhood. "What's up?"

"The kid's pretty shook up, but we got a story from him. Mom is nuts, she's been in and out of the psych hospital. The kid and an older brother, who is—" he consulted his pad, "eighteen, live with her. The older kid's at work. Mom had a gun and was going to shoot herself. The little one, Sam, tried to grab it from her. It went off."

"Ouch," Tony winced, imaging what it must have been like for an eight-year-old. I looked over to Sam, who stood amidst the confusion with tears streaming down his face. My heart went out to him. I left the two still discussing the case and went to Sam.

"It wasn't your fault, you know," I said to him. He looked up at me with tearful eyes.

"I killed her!"

"No Sam, you didn't. You were trying to save her."

He shook his head vehemently, and I wondered how we would get through to him.

"What's going on here?" the voice behind me was a mixture of panic and anger. A tall adolescent with a jacket slung over his shoulder surveyed the scene.

"Sam!" he said, grabbing the boy in a fierce hug. And then he turned to me. "Mom?"

I nodded.

"Did she kill herself? She's been talking about it. I tried to get her to get help, but. . . ."

We talked with the two boys while the ambulance took their mother away and the police finished their work. Dan, the older boy, told me that they had an aunt who he was sure would take them in until some type of arrangements could be made. He seemed to have a positive effect on Sam, who clung to him in quiet desperation. I was sure that this night would haunt the boy for many years, and hoped he could get some help in dealing with it.

By 8:00 we were on our way back to the office to pick up my car, as we had taken Tony's larger one. The boys' aunt had been contacted, and had readily agreed to take them. She ranted about how her sister-in-law should have been put away long ago, but by the time we dropped the boys at her home, she seemed to have calmed herself. I had taken her aside, explaining Sam's feeling that he had killed his mother. I could only hope that she would be sensitive enough to help him let go of his guilt. From her manner, I wasn't sure if she was, but she was family and there was nothing I could do about it. I did suggest that she get him some counseling, to which she had dismissively mumbled, "Sure, sure."

"It's frustrating when you can't save the world," I told Tony, as he pulled into the parking lot of the office. I kept thinking about Sam, wondering how he would make it through the night.

"Ain't it just!" my colleague responded with the same irony. "Was your childhood happy?" he asked unexpectedly.

"Sure, why?"

"Mine, too. Big family. Lots of love. I often wonder why we had it like that and these kids suffer in hell," he shook his head. "Doesn't seem fair, somehow."

I thought of childhoods from hell all weekend, marring what might have been a perfect rest. By Sunday night, I think that Herb was beginning to tire of my worrying about my cases, and we ended the weekend on a bit of a negative note. Protective work can be tough on relationships. I had been told this, and was beginning to understand. I vowed to be more attentive to Herb, and not burden him with my cases in the future.

Monday morning brought a frantic call from Gina. Rudy's daughter, Michelle, had moved in on Saturday, and by Sunday night, her abusive boyfriend had followed her to the house, beat her up, and threatened Gina and the children. Rudy thought that a restraining order should be taken out against him, but Gina had no idea how to do this. I told her how to take Michelle and have her file, but I knew that such orders can have little effect if the perpetrator is determined enough.

"Are you all right?" I asked. "What will you do if he comes back?"

"But he won't if we have the order," Gina responded innocently. I explained to her that a restraining order worked only if the individual in question obeyed it, and if the woman who filed stuck to her guns.

"Oh," said Gina. "I'll tell Rudy."

What telling Rudy was going to do I was not sure. The secretary was buzzing me, and I was not sure what else I could do for Gina. I cautioned her, and asked her to think of a plan whereby everyone would be safe, and told her to call me later.

The secretary told me that there was someone to see me in the lobby. Surprising, as I was expecting no one, but people did occasionally come to the office rather than call. They often had children in tow that they said they could not handle and wanted us to take immediately. I hoped that this was not the case. I was not on intake today, and had come in only to make some calls and catch up on paperwork. There was always a multitude of forms to cover each move that a child made, or any action that we took. Not to keep up-to-date on completing them meant that some foster mother would not get paid, some child could be lost in the paper world, or some other dire consequence that I did not wish to imagine.

In the lobby, I was greeted by the extended hand of a tall, very handsome man who could have walked out of a Brooks Brothers suit commercial. Be still my heart, I thought, until he introduced himself.

"Morris Farley," he told me. "I hear that my wife's sister was here. I wanted to straighten out a few facts for you. May we talk?" Smooth, very smooth.

I found an empty meeting room, a small, windowless cell in which we saw people. The only furnishings were several chairs and a table that supported a phone. These rooms sometimes doubled for makeshift offices when too many social workers happened to be in the office at the same time. I ushered Morris Farley into one of them, and told the receptionist that I did not wish to be disturbed. This would probably be an intense meeting, and I didn't need the phone ringing to interrupt us.

Farley moved as he looked and spoke: smooth. His grooming was impeccable, and a picture of a shack in Maine and three little children huddled around a dying mother flashed through my mind.

"I hear that you met Valerie," began Morris Farley. "A disturbed woman. A very disturbed woman." He shook his head to indicate his sincere sympathy for his sister-in-law.

"I am sure that she told you unthinkable tales. She often does. She has delusions, and we really can't believe much of what she says," he looked pained, as if this poor woman really deserved every bit of understanding that we could muster.

I will admit to being a bit confused. Valerie Anderson had seemed so convincing, and now her brother-in-law seemed even more so. Who was to be believed? The phone's shrill ring startled me. We had no sooner begun when we were already being interrupted.

"Just ignore it," I told my Mr. Farley. "It must be a mistake."

He nodded in acknowledgement, and we both tried to ignore the phone until its insistent ringing ceased.

"My wife died of cancer a week ago," he paused, as if expecting my condolences.

"I am sorry," I said, feeling that I had little choice.

"She was treated for the last year at the Portland Medical Center, but they could do nothing for her. Poor dear. She fought valiantly. Valerie probably told you some tale about a house in the woods. She has mentioned that before. I can't imagine where her deluded mind came up with that."

"I got the impression that the children had told her that," I added, immediately sorry that I had implicated them.

"Oh, I doubt that," said Morris Farley. "They were very happy in their home and school. I can't imagine that they would tell her anything of the sort." He inspected his well-manicured nails, as if in thought. Then he put his hands back in his coat pocket.

"I only asked Valerie to watch the children until I could find a slightly smaller home for them in this area. I thought that it might be better to have them near their aunt and uncle now that poor Denise is gone. I had no idea that Denise's sister would turn against me and not want me to take my children. Especially now," his face was one of mourning again. I was totally confused. He seemed so sincere. The phone shattered the moment. Annoyed now, I picked up and said, perhaps too curtly, "I am in a meeting. Please do not disturb us!"

Morris Farley smiled. "I am sure that you understand that I really need my children at this time of grief. I am returning to Maine briefly today. I am closing out my office there, and will be returning to Massachusetts on Thursday. I hope that I will be able to take my children with me then." He seemed to assume that because he wanted this, I would make it so.

I told him that I would have to look into the case further, and might interview the children, but he seemed not to hear. He was apparently confident that he had successfully pleaded his case and the children would be ready for him on Thursday. There was a lot more that I needed to know before that happened, but I just arranged that we would talk late Wednesday afternoon.

He extended his hand once more when we left the small room, and I noticed the intricately-crafted ring on his finger. A lovely piece of jewelry, it must have cost a good deal. As he started out the door, he turned, and with his hand in his pocket, smiled warmly.

"I am certainly glad I did not have to use this," he said, and was gone. What was that all about, I wondered.

Suddenly, I was barraged by the receptionist and several of my coworkers.

"Are you okay?" they asked breathlessly.

"Sure, why?"

The receptionist was barely able to get her words out, she was so flustered.

"There was a call after you went in to talk to him. It was from the mental health clinic in Portland. They said to call them immediately. They felt that the client you had called them about was homicidal. I didn't know it was him," she indicated the door through which Morris Farley had just passed.

"Then Valerie Anderson called. She was shaken. She said that her brother-in-law had been at her house, demanding the children. She told him that we were involved, and he took off. She said that he had a gun in his pocket and was gunning for the social worker. I put two and two together. But we were afraid if we barged in, we'd drive him to something. Oh, I'm so glad you're alright."

Now it was my turn to be flustered. I imagined Morris Farley patting his pocket, and I realized what he was glad that he had not had to use.

Polly Stern came rushing into the lobby.

"Are you okay?" the question of the hour.

Once I had composed myself, I called the mental health center.

"We had to let you know that he is dangerous," the therapist told me. "He is quite delusional, a paranoid schizophrenic. He's supposed to be on medication, but he refuses to take it." He explained further that while usually they could not give out that much information about a client, the fact that he had tried to kill one of their therapists made this an exception. In fact, the contact told me, there was a warrant out for his arrest in Maine. They had not been able to catch him. I told the therapist about Farley's plans to return to Maine to close out his office.

"He said he is going back today," I explained.

"Can you sit tight? I'd like to have the police call you back for more details."

Within a few minutes, I was describing the interchange with Morris Farley to the Maine police, who told me that they planned to pick him up as soon as possible. Valerie Anderson had just gained back her believability. An interview with the children later in the day confirmed that it was Morris, not Valerie, who was delusional. The police were able to intercept the children's father, and he was arrested for the attempted murder of a therapist at the mental health center. Several days later, I assisted Valerie and Dick Anderson in getting legal guardianship of the Farley children. I hoped that finally the lives of these children could be transformed into the happy childhoods that they deserved.

Questions for Thought _____

1. What were your initial reactions to Valerie Anderson's story? How might you have handled it?

2. How would you have reacted when Gina told you that she was pregnant? What thoughts might have gone through your mind?

3. How would you have felt about Michelle moving in with the family?

4. How would you have felt when Sam called? How would you have handled the situation?

5. Other than those he expressed, what feelings might Sam have had in the face of his mother's death? How might you have helped him?

6. What was your initial impression of Morris Farley? How might you have handled the case?

7. How would you have felt after the interview with Mr. Farley?

22

Happy Endings

A call from Gina several days later was welcome. I had been worried about her, and had thought I should call numerous times, but the work load had been such that it never seemed possible.

"Michelle's gone," Gina started, and I began to fear the worst.

"She went back to her mother's in Utah. She figured, as far away from this guy that she could get, the better," I breathed a sigh of relief. I had no idea what kind of a mother Rudy's second wife was, but I was thankful that Michelle was out of harm and that Gina and Rudy's home would once again be relatively tranquil.

"Are you coming out soon? I miss seeing you," Gina and I had grown fond of each other, and it was difficult to remember boundaries. I also knew that with Trudy's death, her children's custody would remain with their father, and we would be closing the case. I had told Gina that and her calls had increased. Nothing major, just a need to touch base. I guessed that I was the first woman in Gina's life with whom she could identify. Certainly those in her neighborhood were not good candidates, and she was estranged from her own mother. Had I become a mother figure at barely thirty?

"I'll be out as soon as I can, Gina, but we do have to close your case, you know," I tried to sound firm but kind.

"I know," she said sadly. "Can I still talk to you, afterward, I mean?" I wondered what the Department would say, but I didn't care.

"Sure," I answered, and she seemed relieved.

"I want to ask you something. When this baby's born, I'm thinking of getting my tubes tied. What do you think?" I hesitated, not sure how to respond. Actually, I thought it was a great idea. Gina would have seven children to raise, and that seemed like enough for anyone, but I also knew how important her children were to her.

"Let's talk about it when I come out," I suggested, and we made a date for a visit.

It was difficult to say goodbye to Gina officially, and there was a heavy feeling in my heart as I stopped in front of her house. It had been months since I had promised to come out, and appointments to visit had to be cancelled again and again as the work piled up. Gina seemed understanding, and our frequent phone contacts obviously helped. I wondered if some unconscious motivation had made me cancel appointments because I couldn't handle closing her case. That was quite possible. I knew that she wanted to keep in touch. I had run it by Polly, my supervisor, who wasn't crazy about the idea of a social worker keeping in touch with a client after the case was closed. But she also recognized that Gina needed the support, and suggested that I keep our relationship within some boundaries.

Gina heard my car and came out to greet me. She was well into her pregnancy, and looking fit and happy. Trudy's death had removed quite a burden from her shoulders. The family downstairs had finally been evicted, and both Rudy and Gina were glad to see new couple move in. Although I had not met them, Gina's description suggested that she might have found a friend in the wife.

"I was afraid you'd cancel again," she told me as she let me in. I felt guilty, though I doubted that she intended it as the comment had sounded. She had redecorated the small kitchen, and I commented on it. She beamed with satisfaction.

"I did this for you," she said shyly, handing me a drawing of a woods scene. She knew how much I loved the woods, and that I would escape there whenever possible. It was a beautiful drawing, worthy to be hung in any house.

"That's so you don't forget me," she said, pointing to a small figure that I hadn't even noticed perched in the hollow of a tree. It was a tiny fairy. Gina, the lover of fairies, had wanted me to have a part of her. I was deeply touched, and my eyes began to smart with the threat of tears.

We talked comfortably in the warm kitchen, mindless of anything but the bond we felt between us. I wondered if Gina and I would have been friends had we met in another way or in another time. Or was it just that I had seen her in the context of her life, in contrast to so many others who were not coping as well? Was it her courage that endeared her to me? I would never know.

I left Gina for the last time officially with a bittersweet feeling, glad that she had reached a point where the Department could close her case, but grieving about an important relationship that was formally ending. Gina asked again if she could call, and I agreed, but we both knew that it would not be quite the same.

I had scheduled a visit to Tammy Howard's foster home the same day, deciding that I needed this day of positive contacts to compensate for the terribly severe cases we had been encountering in Intake lately. Buoyed by my visit with Gina, I turned down the Howards' street with anticipation. Two little girls, who I recognized as Lissy and Ellen, were playing in the fenced-in yard. I was amazed at the changes in Lissy. Dark and enchanting, she darted about with a grace that would have eluded her when we had first met. Ellen, almost two years older than Lissy, had adopted a motherly attitude that I recognized as mirroring her big sister, Terri. Tammy joined them as I watched the two little girls and marveled at how far they had come. We chatted for a few minutes about the children and how well they played together.

"When do you think they will hear the adoption petition?" asked Tammy. We had filed to have Mava Melanson's parental rights terminated so that Lissy could be placed for adoption. Because she had bonded so well with the foster mother, the adoption worker had explored adoption with the Howards. But Tammy's husband's company was threatening layoffs, and they both felt that adopting a child at this time would be unfair. I guessed, though, that Tammy would hate to see Lissy go.

"Terri's really upset about her being placed for adoption, too," said the foster mother. I heard the 'too' and my thoughts that the adoptive placement with a strange family was a reality that Tammy, herself, was dreading, were confirmed. "She'll be home any minute. She asked if you could stay and see her."

I had taken Terri out numerous times since she had come to the Howards' foster home. I felt that she needed a sounding board to sort out her feelings about her mother and the life they could have had. Irene had still not remained sober, and I doubted that she ever would. There had been talk of petition for the termination of parental rights for Ellen and the two younger boys, but we had not proceeded as yet. I was not sure how Terri would take this, and thought we should go slowly. There was a possibility the boys' foster home might want to adopt, and I felt that that would work out well. Howie was still in residential treatment, and it was unlikely that he would be released soon. Irene's instability had taken its toll on him. I found it interesting that Howie and his sister Terri had reacted so differently. Was it Terri's opportunities to mother the younger siblings that had made her feel more in control, and therefore able to deal with the family dysfunction better? Was Howie more vulnerable because he felt out of control, and as a male in our culture, found that totally unacceptable? It was hard to tell. Today, with the increased interest in the resiliency of traumatized children, some might say that Terri was just more resilient for whatever reason. Whatever the underlying causes, I felt that Terri would be okay.

"Sure," I told the foster mother. "I can wait for her. I haven't taken her out alone for a few weeks. It might be good for her."

Tammy smiled and nodded. She had grown very fond of the teen, but I knew that the young foster mother was not sure how to explain Irene to the girl. In fact, I knew that Tammy found it unbelievable that, as a mother, Irene would choose her addiction over her children.

"Come on in," said Tammy finally. "I have some hot water for tea. I know that you prefer that to coffee." How well she had learned my little habits.

We chatted about the girls and their progress.

"You know," she said finally. "Terri has a home here for as long as she likes. And Ellen, too, although you probably will want to place her for adoption. I hope that Terri could visit. I think anything else would break her heart."

The door burst open at that point, and an excited Terri barreled into the room.

"I saw your car! Great, you waited. I wanted to show you my report card," she beamed, thrusting a rumpled card at me. I exclaimed about her A's and B's.

"Great job! I'm proud of you. I think that deserves an ice cream break. What do you think?" Terri smiled, and I knew that she was pleased at the suggestion. She was so grown up, but at the Howards' she had also been allowed to be a child again. It had done wonders for her.

We drove a short distance to a shop that had ice cream, and we took our cones outside to enjoy the last of the warm fall days.

"I've been doing some thinking," said the teen. I knew that no response was required, so we sat in silence for a moment while Terri seemed to compose her thoughts.

"If I keep my high school grades up, Tammy says that the Department has scholarships for kids like me. Is that true?"

I nodded, "Yes, it is."

"Well, I want to go to college." It was a pronouncement that seemed to take courage for her to make. No one in her family had finished high school, let alone gone to college, and I am sure that she wondered if she could do it.

"That's great! I loved college. I'll bet you will, too."

"Do you know what I want to study?" she asked.

"I am all ears," I replied, smiling at her seriousness.

Terri looked at me for a long moment, and then looked down. I realized that she was blushing.

"I want to be a social worker," she said, almost inaudibly.

I could feel my eyes filling with tears for the second time that day. I had no doubt that she was identifying with me, and I was deeply touched.

She went on, "And maybe I will work with kids, and with alcoholic mothers." There were tears in her eyes as well, and I knew that if she could not save Irene, she hoped that someday she could help another child's mom.

"I'm glad," I finally answered. "I think you will be a great social worker!"

That night, as I went about my tasks at home, I still felt the warmth of my connection with both Terri and Gina. Protective Services work is not always easy and often not rewarding. But when the rewards come, they seem to be even more important. I learned over my years in work with maltreated children to appreciate the little things and to value the smallest efforts that clients might make. The flowers amidst the filth. But when on the same day, two people who had been through so much had touched me in a special manner, I decided that I could never be more blessed. All the other unpleasant moments seemed worth it.

The glow got me through the next day on Intake when again the phones were unusually busy. A father, in the act of beating his wife and threatening her with a butcher knife, had accidentally wounded his seven-year-old son. The boy was hospitalized, and the hospital refused to release him and called us. Later in the day, the same hospital notified us that they had a baby that had been born addicted to heroin. Such cases were and still are mandatory reports to child protection. Another case for me to investigate. In the meantime, I had to find a foster home for the baby, not always an easy task. Addicted babies are often irritable and difficult to care for. Not all foster mothers could handle the problems that might result from the baby's small system having been overtaxed by drugs.

It was mid-morning when I finally got a break. I was walking to the break room when I glanced into the workers' main room and saw a familiar face.

"Zach! What are you doing here?" He was putting some papers and books into a desk.

"Well, hello yourself!" he answered. "I wondered when I would see you."

"What are you doing?"

"Moving in!" he said with a chuckle. "You just seemed to be having too much fun! I was jealous." Herb and Zach were still friends, and since Herb and I had started dating, we often had visits from Zach or double-dated with him and his current flame. But for the last few months, Herb and I had both been so busy at our individual jobs that we had been at Herb's place very little. In fact, we had not seen Zach for two months, now that I thought about it. He must have put in a transfer that long ago, but he had never said a word.

"Adoption too tame? Just wait!" I joked. "Hey, can you take a break? I was just headed that way."

I was pleased to have Zach in this office. His refreshing sense of humor would be a balm when things got too tough.

"You're a fink for not telling us you were transferring," I told him over my tea.

"I can't give away all my secrets!" he countered with his usual laugh.

"Well, I hope you got those seat covers for your car. You'll need them!" I teased, telling him then about the lice-infested and dirty children that I had had to transport in my car.

Zach grimaced. "Ugh! I wonder if I can transfer back to adoption?"

Zach fit in well and learned quickly. I would actually work with him on a particularly difficult case later in the year. I was glad that it was my old friend with me on that one. We reminisced about children that ate ties and new cars rolling down the hill, and somehow the case did not seem so difficult.

Questions for Thought

1. When is it acceptable to maintain contact with a client after a case is closed? When would it be unwise?

2. How would you have responded to Gina's question about having a tubal ligation? What might you have said?

3. How do you personally deal with endings? How might this affect your clients?

4. What do you think about the Howards' decision not to adopt Lissy? What might have been the pros and cons of such an adoption?

5. Why do you think Terri and Howie turned out so differently?

6. How might you help foster parents understand abusive parents?

23

Seasons of Change

Fall merged into winter and the snowfall was exceptionally heavy that year. Schools and events were cancelled, but it never seemed to deter people from abusing and neglecting their children. Some of my colleagues postulated that the snow actually contributed to the abuse rate when parents were cooped up with children all the time. But when winter became spring and spring slid into summer, parents continued to abuse and neglect children, and we remained busy in the Intake unit. No matter how long I covered protective cases, it never got easier to witness the scars that parents caused their children. My occasional card from an old adoptive client helped to assure me that there were happy endings sometimes. And there were some parents who had gotten it together and were able to care for their children. A successfully closed case also made for a great feeling.

I got a call from Gina from time to time, though not as frequently as we had both anticipated. She had taken an art class at an adult education program and promised to send me a picture. Betty Jane was doing much better, and they had found a special school for Mercy Ann. Gina said that her two babies were growing, and couldn't I come to see them sometime? I promised that I would, but never quite made it.

It was early in the fall that I received a message that Gina had called. I had not heard from her all summer, so I assumed she was busy and doing well. The message was marked "important" and I prayed that nothing was wrong. But it was a cheerful Gina who answered the phone.

"Oh, I am glad that you called back!" she said cheerily. "I wondered if you could do me a favor?"

"If I can. What is it?" I tried to sound like I would love to help her out.

She paused for a moment, and I realized that it was self-consciousness.

"Rudy and I thought that maybe . . . That it was time . . . We want to get married, and we wanted to know if you could stand up for us!" Of all that I expected, this was the furthest from anything I had imagined. I knew that both of them had been badly hurt in their previous marriages, and I had doubted that they would ever marry again, even each other. But apparently their bond of trust had grown to the point that each was able to take a chance again. I was sure that this union would last.

A myriad of thoughts ran through my head in the millisecond that I hesitated. One thought was how honored I felt, and at the same time, I thought how sad it was that this couple had no one closer to them than a former social worker with whom to share their special moment.

"I'd be honored," I answered quickly, hoping that my hesitation had not been obvious to Gina.

"I know that you are not married but do you, I mean, if you want to bring anyone. Well, we need two people, the Justice of the Peace said, and . . ."

"Sure, I have someone who would love to come," I assured her. Things had been a bit rocky between Herb and me lately. My job was taxing my energies and we had been growing apart, but I was sure that he would do this for me.

"We're just going to go on Friday night. I got a baby sitter and we just thought we'd go and do it."

I imagined all the extravagant weddings my friends had been having, even those people who had been married before. And here were Gina and Rudy, neither of whom had probably ever had a big wedding, stealing away to a Justice of the Peace on a Friday night as if it were a casual trip to the movies.

"Let us take you out to dinner," I said spontaneously. "We can celebrate."

"Oh," she began, seeming stunned. "I guess, I mean, yes, I'd like that!" she had brightened, and I imagined that the event was beginning to take on more excitement for her.

"What time is the Justice of the Peace available?"

"He said the latest he could do it is 6:00. He and his wife are going out later."

"Great," I told her. "I'll make reservations for 7:00. Okay?"

"Yes," said Gina excitedly. "I'll call Rudy now!"

I wondered what people here at the office would say, and reasoned that Gina was no longer my client. I mentioned it to Polly, just to get a reading, and she seemed pleased.

"When folks get it together, I always feel like celebrating! Have a great time."

I had a variety of feelings as Herb and I rang the bell at the Justice of the Peace's house. This particular official apparently had a room in his home set aside for weddings. His wife answered the door and beamed as she let us in.

"The happy couple is already here," she explained. "They are talking over the details with my husband. You must be the witnesses. Come right this way." And she ushered us into the wedding room.

The first floor room might have once been a study or den. Now it was decorated predominately in white, with a little trellis at one end and plants around the room. There was a fragrance of flowers as we entered, and I thanked this thoughtful couple for adorning Gina and Rudy's simple wedding with the lovely array of blooms that were placed about the room. Herb looked at me and smiled as Mrs. Justice of the Peace bustled off to some other duty.

"Pretty, huh?" I agreed that it was.

Gina and Rudy came in soon after. She was carrying a lovely small bouquet that she sniffed periodically, enjoying its fragrance. A gift from Rudy, she told me later. She wore a simple dress in pale green that complemented her complexion and eyes. I had never seen Rudy in anything but work clothes, and the transformation created by his dark suit was amazing. Was he standing a little straighter and looking a bit more confident?

The ceremony was brief, and I was surprised at how touched Rudy was by it. I always thought of him as the silent, unemotional type, but there were tears in his eyes as well as in Gina's. When they sealed their union with a kiss, I felt teary, too. How much these two had come through to reach where they were tonight.

I had chosen an attractive restaurant with a dining room that was decorated with huge plants and several fountains. Gina reminded me of a country girl gaping at the sights of the big city as she gazed around her in awe.

"This is beautiful," she breathed. "I just want to . . ." she couldn't seem to find the words, and finally said, ". . . paint it!" We all laughed. The artist had come into her own.

I will always remember that dinner celebration with Gina and Rudy. It felt so good to see them feeling like celebrities for the evening. It was certainly not part of their usual lives. Gina had taught me so much about the simple elegance of the human spirit, and how much some people have to give. I still think of her many years later, and wonder where she is and what path her life has taken. I hope that Rudy is treating her well, and that the children are doing well. I am honored to have been part of an important moment in her life.

Little did I know that night, that as Gina and Rudy began a new life together, my relationship with Herb would be ending. Several days later, we ended our long relationship and parted as friends. I heard about him from Zach, and will admit to a twinge of sadness when, almost a year later, he married someone else.

I was tiring of the constant strain of the Intake Unit. Tony had transferred units again, as had several of my other colleagues, and things did not seem quite the same. I considered going into foster care homefinding, but in the meantime, helped out with some training sessions in the absence of the regular trainer. I loved the experience, and when the trainer for the Central Region left some months later, I applied for the position and got it.

For several years, I would find satisfaction in training new workers as they came on the job, idealistic and eager to save the world. I like to think that I helped to temper some of their idealism and transform it into the appreciation of the strengths that clients bring, even though crisis might temporarily hide their potential. It is perhaps not surprising that after marrying and beginning my own family, I would graduate from training to teaching potential social workers.

When my students ask me, "what was it really like out there?" my mind returns to Gina, Terri, Skipper, Billy, and all the children and parents in whose lives I hope I made a difference. As I recount these memories, I realize that I have changed, too. I have learned that social work is not just the mechanical manipulation of people's lives.

Instead, it is an opportunity to explore our own inner potential as we reach out a hand to help others on paths that might be rockier than our own. What a challenge, but what a gift!

Questions for Thought

1. How would you feel if a former client asked you to be a witness at his or her wedding? What thoughts might run through your mind?

2. How might you have felt at a wedding like Gina's and Rudy's? How did it compare with the weddings of your family or friends?

3. As you look back on the career depicted here, what would have made the most impression on you? Why?

4. What case would have been the most difficult for you? Why?

5. Have you formulated any plans for your own career after reading this account?